# THE
# MEDITERRANEAN
# GARDENER

# THE
# MEDITERRANEAN
# GARDENER

## HUGO LATYMER

With photographs by Niccolò Grassi

FRANCES LINCOLN
in association with
THE ROYAL BOTANIC GARDENS, KEW

**To Jinty**

Frances Lincoln Limited
4 Torriano Mews, Torriano Avenue
London NW5 2RZ

*The Mediterranean Garden*
Copyright © Frances Lincoln Limited 1990
Text copyright © Hugo Latymer 1990

First Frances Lincoln edition: 1990
First paperback edition: 2001

British Library Cataloguing-in-Publication Data
A catalogue record for this book is available
from the British Library

ISBN 0 7112 1828 5

Printed and bound in China
by CS Graphics

5 7 9 8 6 4

*Frances Lincoln Ltd acknowledge the assistance of the
Royal Botanic Gardens, Kew, in the preparation of this book.*

# CONTENTS

# FOREWORD

Mrs Martineau complained as early as 1924 that 'though there have been many botanical books on Mediterranean . . . flora, the scattered knowledge of the Riviera horticulturists . . . has never been gathered up in any practical manual.'

The book that she wrote, *Gardening in Sunny Lands*, admirably corrected that deficiency. However, the practice of gardening has progressed a long way in sixty years and few practical guides have since been produced expressly for the large and popular Mediterranean region. In this book I have tried to fill the gap: to offer some guidance on the practice of gardening and to gather together notes on plant material for the benefit of those living in, or visiting, regions favoured by hot, dry summers and mild, wet winters.

Perhaps the greatest change that has taken place since Mrs Martineau's day is the summer migration from cooler to warmer climates. Sixty years ago people, like swallows, moved to the Mediterranean almost exclusively for the months of winter. When Mrs Martineau wrote her book she was concerned with the appearance of the garden between Christmas and Easter. No person in their right mind, she thought, would consider the possibility of remaining for the dreadful heat of summer, if they could possibly avoid it.

Today there has been a complete about-turn. Garden designers now plan for colourful summer displays of oleanders, bougainvilleas and hibiscus and are far more interested in shrubs that flower in summer and autumn than were their predecessors, whose winter and spring gardens gave prominence to bulbs, almonds and mimosas. Palms are now a major constituent of the garden whereas, in 1924, Mrs Martineau wrote: 'In many of the newer gardens the palms are being uprooted and either sold or burned. They are still in demand but a keen gardener will seldom be willing to spare the ground for them.'

On the other hand, the essential form of the Mediterranean garden has not changed much. The herbaceous border is hardly to be found, even though a number of herbaceous plants can easily be grown. Gardening in the English sense – of making a garden of many different kinds of plants – has never caught on. Instead, the typical Mediterranean garden remains essentially architectural: water, walls, paths, steps and statuary are important components.

In choosing garden plants to recommend I have, on the whole, concentrated on those plants that are available at local nurseries. To provide an opportunity for sallying a short way into the realms of the unusual, I have also included a few more exotic varieties that can easily be raised from seed. However, though there is interest, and sometimes even satisfaction, in experimenting with little-known varieties, it is important to recognize that the plants that will grow best under your conditions are those that you will see in the hills and wild places of your own neighbourhood, rather than imported species that require dedicated effort to grow successfully. Rosemary, cistus, broom, pistachio, arbutus, these, and other indigenous plants, are the species perfectly adapted to your garden, the ones that will survive without watering in summer, and reward you with their vigour if given a little fertilizer and the occasional summer soaking.

This book is, to some extent, a scrapbook of other people's scraps, for most that one learns in this existence is derived from other people's experiences. Learning in general, however, is made harder by the fact that it is possible to find totally opposing views on any subject – so perhaps the art of life lies in making a correct choice from among the contradictions. When my experience has been slight on any point, my choices have been guided by the books acknowledged in the bibliography.

# THE CLIMATE

Broadly speaking, this book caters for gardeners living in warm temperate regions that experience four months of hot, almost totally dry summer weather and wet but sunny winters, with lowest annual temperatures of between 2°C/35°F and −6°C/21°F. As well as in the regions bordering the Mediterranean Sea, such conditions are to be found in parts of central and southern California, in South Africa's western Cape Province, in parts of southern, western and eastern Australia and along some of the coast of Chile.

Since any definition must draw limits across steady gradations of climate, the boundaries will always be rather arbitrary. However, one of the most practical ways to define climatic boundaries is by the distribution of native 'indicator plants'. The plant most often used to define Mediterranean conditions is the olive; but olives can resist temperatures as low as −10°C/14°F, well below the minimum normally experienced along most of the Mediterranean coast. It is probably more useful to think in terms of the warmer areas where oranges will grow: the orange will not endure a minimum temperature that falls much below −6°C/21°F.

It is important to recognize that altitude has a significant effect on temperature. Every 200m/650ft rise in altitude gives a consequent drop of 1°C/1.8°F in temperature. Thus even gardens situated at no great altitude may experience temperatures that, throughout the year, are 2-3°C/3-5°F cooler than sites only a short distance away.

Lower temperatures may make it rather easier to grow some plants that do not like summer heat, but the difference of these few degrees is felt most acutely in the tolerance to winter minimum temperatures. There are many plants that will not mind an occasional frost of −1°C/30°F but will die at −4°C/25°F. On the French Riviera, at Cannes, for instance, you will find gardens by the sea, in protected places, that see a slight frost only once in every five to ten years, while in the hills around Grasse, only a few kilometres inland, temperatures fall as low as −8°C/17°F almost every year. There are hilly regions of California – the Pasadena foothills, for example – that experience frosts in most years.

However, in a Mediterranean climate, it is drought rather than cold that presents a hazard to plant life. Fortunately it is possible, to a large extent, to alleviate dry conditions by watering – at least, this is possible for those who have a good supply of water.

By a good supply I mean one that will not disappear just when it is most needed – at the peak of summer – and also one that is relatively free of dissolved salts, which, even in weak solution, are harmful to plants. In many coastal areas the increased use of water because of tourism has drawn sea water into the aquifers and has increased salinity to levels which few plants will accept. Water that has passed through those types of water softener that are regenerated from common salt is also sodium-rich and inimical to healthy plant growth. If you have no alternative but to use salty water, you should choose those plants that are specially adapted to saline coastal conditions and give preference to those that are drought resistant too. If, on the other hand, you are determined to have a garden of verdant lawns, green foliage and bright flowers, you will have to provide a source of pure water and an efficient system of applying it regularly and economically (the basic options for methods of watering are outlined on pages 140-149).

Without an adequate supply of pure water you will experience great difficulty in creating any garden that looks green in summer, for all the plants that are naturally resistant to long drought take a rest at this time of year, and they become, on the whole, rather desiccated and grey. In extreme drought some may even become summer-deciduous and shed all their leaves, in exactly the same way that cold-climate trees survive the desiccating effects of frost and wind by dropping their leaves in winter. The almond, for instance, is partly summer-deciduous: it blossoms in late winter and immediately breaks into foliage so it can make sufficient growth before its leaves become shrivelled by the heat of high summer.

Aerial humidity is another factor of great importance, though we often fail to take it into consideration – perhaps because we cannot see it. There are places in the world (the tops of hills in the Galapagos islands, for example) that have almost no rainfall but support lush vegetation because of the high humidity. In a Mediterranean summer not only the rainfall but also the aerial humidity is very low. A large number of species indigenous to regions that experience summer drought, and quite a few from elsewhere, have strategies for coping with the dry months: annuals simply die back once they have scattered their seeds; other plants retire into bulbs, rhizomes or corms; and others develop leaf hairs or thick skins that reduce evaporation.

One consequence of this natural plant behaviour, and one of the distinct characteristics of Mediterranean gardening, is the 'second spring'. Because frost can occur well into the months of early spring, and the dry heat of summer follows on very rapidly, the real spring is often condensed into little more than a month. At the other end of the year, however, there is a long period, from the arrival of the first rains until the first really cold spell of winter, when conditions for plant growth are excellent. Except in deciduous trees and shrubs, almost as much growth is seen at this time as in spring. Roses bloom, orange trees colour up their fruit; many plants are busy growing and flowering well into the winter months. So early autumn is a moment to concentrate on, the time for most of your planting and some fertilizing, as well as the pruning of those trees and shrubs that have not been watered during the summer and are still in a resting state.

Another marked characteristic of gardening in a dry climate is the cultivation of plants in pots. In regions that experience more frequent rainfall, plants in the open ground will prosper without too much attention. In dry summer conditions all plants but the most drought-resistant need frequent watering, and the quantities of scarce and expensive water that are absorbed, even in a small garden, become considerable. The use of containers, limiting the area of soil that needs to be watered, cuts down on both water consumption and the labour of watering.

While summer aridity is perhaps the principal factor determining the choice of plants to grow, there are other limiting conditions. Winter cold rules out all tropical plants and, except in a few chosen places, those subtropical plants that will not stand a frost. Another significant factor is the intensity of the sunlight. Many plants wilt in direct sun, and you will need to bear this in mind when choosing plants, especially for those parts of the garden that are fully exposed to the sun when it is directly overhead during the middle of the day.

The high winds that are prevalent in many of the areas with a Mediterranean climate dry up both plant foliage and the soil, and can snap the branches off even well-established trees. If your garden is subject to wind, you should plant trees to protect the exposed sides.

The climate can affect the quality of the soil in other ways. Summer drought hinders the formation of humus and the microflora that make a rich soil. In some areas this problem has been compounded by overgrazing, so that soil is almost devoid of plant foods. However, such soils often react magnificently to applications of a complete fertilizer.

Remember, too, that many dry regions have alkaline soil, partly because of the geological structure, but also because drought inhibits the decay of vegetation: it is vegetable decay which, in regions of high rainfall, encourages acidity. Consequently, the information given in this book is somewhat biased towards gardening on calcareous soil. Acid-loving plants have not been entirely ignored, however, as they can of course be grown in pots or raised beds as long as these are filled with specially prepared soil.

## CREATING A MEDITERRANEAN CLIMATE
In colder regions, an approximation to Mediterranean conditions can be artificially created, without much expense or trouble, in a greenhouse or conservatory: you need only maintain high daytime temperatures and low humidity in summer, and provide just enough heating to keep out frosts in winter. The low summer humidity is particularly important, since the ability to resist cold depends not just on the degree of frost but also on the hardness of the growth on which it falls. The fast, soft growth that is encouraged by moist conditions is not likely to be able to withstand a long cold spell in winter.

## MEDITERRANEAN GARDENING IN THE BRITISH ISLES
Many gardeners in the British Isles are fortunate enough to live in areas where the winter temperature seldom falls as low as −6°C/21°F. However, few of these areas can be considered truly Mediterranean in climate, nor will the majority of the plants described in this book thrive there. The climate of Cornwall, the west coast of Wales, the Irish coast and the Western Isles of Scotland is protected from frost by the Gulf Stream but is generally quite dull and wet, encouraging soft, sappy plant growth and preventing adequate ripening of the wood of tender trees and shrubs. The south coast of England from South Devon eastwards to Sussex is rather more Mediterranean with lower rainfall and more sunlight; here some of the planting described in this book becomes a possibility, at least in sheltered microclimates or against a south or south-west facing wall. Central London, made a couple of degrees warmer by the heat of the city and with chilling winds slowed down by the roughness of its surface, also allows much Mediterranean-style planting to survive.

# MEDITERRANEAN GARDENS

A variety of attractive and practical design solutions have arisen in response to the particular demands of gardening in climates with hot, dry summers and mild, wet winters. Most demonstrate a successful compromise between the needs of the gardener – or indeed anyone who is to enjoy the garden – and the plants in their care.

They have evolved over centuries of gardening experience as the most practical and congenial solutions to the problems of providing shade – principally for human beings – and water – principally for plants – in the months of summer heat and drought.

Each individual will clearly have a different approach to creating a garden. But when planning one remember that it should not be a chore, but a joy to sustain it. Be clear before you start about the use it will be put to and how much time you will devote both to enjoying and to maintaining your precious outdoor space.

Cool courtyards built round gently cascading fountains, tiled patios with dappled shade from overhead vines, terraced slopes left wild with sweet smelling cistus and rosemary or planted with drought-resistant cacti or succulents – these are solutions that please the eye, engage the intellect and refresh the spirit. The following pages explore a variety of styles and approaches.

# CHOOSING A STYLE

The impact on design of the two great garden styles of the western Mediterranean region has been immense. The first, the Moorish, seen at its most sublime in the gardens of the Alhambra in Granada and the Alcazar in Seville, is based on the traditional Islamic garden. In this the garden was divided by waterways – representing the four Rivers of Life – into four, the quadripartite design which has been echoed in gardens throughout the western world. The style came to Spain with the Moors from North Africa.

The second style, vastly different in concept, is that of the Italian Renaissance where the emphasis is on balance and proportion. Full of statuary, impressive balustrades, terraces, flights of steps, fountains and basins, these gardens are dramatic and formal.

While the Moorish style is intimate, designed for people to use and devoid of statuary or ornament, the Italian Renaissance garden is made to amaze, to be wondered at and admired. Both styles have been adopted and adapted in countries way beyond the Mediterranean region. The Islamic influence, for example, is evident not only in the gardens of the Taj Mahal but, through the conquistadors, in gardens of South America. The influence of the great Italian gardens spread first to France, where it is much in evidence at Versailles, and then to Britain where it can be seen, for example, in the gardens of Powis Castle in Wales. Italian influences are also apparent in the relatively recent gardens at Blake House in California.

Present-day gardeners can rarely afford to emulate the flamboyance of the Italian High Renaissance, though elements of it are evident in details – fountains, statuary, ornament – of gardens throughout the world. The Moorish style is far more accessible and practical. Here we see the earthly manifestation of the Paradise Garden promised to the faithful in the Koran – a place where 'spreading shade', 'fountains of running water' and 'cool pavilions' offer delight and refreshment.

**Far left** The fourfold division of the traditional Islamic garden is evident in the arrangement of the tiled paths leading to a central raised fountain in the courtyard garden of the Palacio de las Dueñas in Seville. The courtyard is an ancient garden form.

**Left** The Italian Garden at Blake House, Kensington, California, was inspired by one at Frascati, near Rome. The Blake House gardens successfully 'translate' the principles of Italianate garden design in the context of the New World.

**Above** Elegant yet undemanding planting makes this pergola in a Santa Barbara garden a design feature in its own right. The geometry of the brick-paved path complements the strong, sculptural lines of the yuccas.

# COURTYARD GARDENS

Separate courtyards and hedge-enclosed divisions that often bear little relationship to one another or to any obvious ground plan are typical of the Moorish gardens in southern Spain. They reflect the influence of a desert people for whom small enclosures – if only a tent – provided welcome refuge from the heat and perils of a vast uninviting desert.

Similarly, in the Mediterranean regions of Europe, the Middle East and the western United States, courtyards provide privacy and shade, respite from the relentless heat of the midday sun. The contrast between this haven and the heat and dust of the surrounding countryside is made all the more delightful by the introduction of water. Bubbling up in a bowl, cascading from a small fountain, lying deep, dark and still in a central well or simply reflecting the surrounding court, its very presence refreshes the spirit.

When designing your garden, then, do bear in mind the advantages of creating an enclosed, shady oasis. You are sure to yearn for it in the scorching heat of high

summer. Such an area is quite inexpensive to establish and very easy to maintain. Nor does it demand a lot of space. You can, for example, pave an area as small as 5 m sq/30 sq yd, and surround it with a hedge of Italian cypress (*Cupressus sempervirens*). Pierce the hedge with arched entrances and place a couple of comfortable benches within. Add, if you wish, a container-grown flowering shrub and a small raised pond (see page 42).

You can work endless variations on this theme, enclosing the courtyard with a wall rather than a hedge, and using the wall to support a colourful climber. Create an interesting pattern of tiles or bricks for the floor area (you will find some ideas for this on pages 30-33) and choose from the vast range of garden furniture the style best suited to your setting – whether in wrought iron, wood or one of the excellent modern plastics. If the overall effect is harmonious, you will find yourself retreating to sit in this tranquil spot far more frequently than you may ever have imagined.

If your garden is large enough, you could consider dividing it into a number of different, highly individual areas, each one separately enclosed within walls or hedges. Depending on whether you use sombre evergreens such as the Italian cypress or flowering species such as *Viburnum tinus*, and whether you make your enclosures rigidly geometric or flowingly curvaceous, you can achieve a range of effects from the impressively formal to the enchantingly casual.

Try to make each individual area distinct, so that you experience a sense of novelty and surprise as you move from one to the other. You could give each of these 'garden rooms' a separate theme. One, for example, might be devoted entirely to plants of a single colour – white petunias and pelargoniums look wonderful set against a cypress hedge – or to plants from a single family, such as the roses.

**Left** Cool grey walls and paving in this enclosed courtyard garden contrast with the brilliant hues of bougainvillea and the strident scarlet blooms of a pot-grown ornamental pomegranate (*Punica granatum*).

**Right** Simplicity is the keynote in the entrance to this inviting Mediterranean 'oasis'. The success of this design depends almost entirely on striking contrasts of colours, forms and textures.

Warm ochre-rust coloured walls provide the perfect backdrop for the deep dense green of the planting in the courtyard of a 16th-century Sicilian farmhouse. Cacti and succulents do well here: water is not readily available and summer temperatures may soar to 40°C (104°F).

# PATIO GARDENS

The very fact that the Mediterranean climate is so equable and agreeable means that land in the areas that enjoy it is highly priced. Few people, whether permanent residents or second-home owners, have pockets deep enough or areas large enough for extensive gardens. Together with the particular merits of enclosing space described in Courtyard Gardens, this fact makes the patio a highly attractive and practical proposition.

The patio has a very long history, dating back to Roman times when well-heeled citizens built their residences around a central *atrium* – an open court. The area might be graced by a central fountain, and was used as an extension of the house which gave onto it. Thus it would be used for relaxation or for taking meals in fine weather. The tradition was carried across Europe by Roman legionaries and found its way to Spain in the courtyards of the Arab conquerors from North Africa. Though the concepts were originally virtually identical, today the terms patio and courtyard are not synonymous.

Here we shall consider the patio principally as a paved area providing a formal or informal link with the house, and serving, in effect, as an 'outdoor living room'. In California the same purpose is likely to be served by the wooden deck.

## CHOOSING A SITE

If you are starting from scratch you may well have a choice of sites for a patio. However, quite apart from the fact that siting it next to the house makes sense in terms of convenience and accessibility, this may well be the best spot in terms of land use. If you have engaged in any moderately extensive construction or reconstruction, the area immediately adjacent to the house is probably the one in which the builders dumped their waste. The soil will inevitably have been affected and it is far easier to pave over such an area than to attempt to improve it.

Before you choose a site you should also consider carefully how you will use the patio. Unless you are primarily interested in sunbathing, a site that gets the sun earlier in the day is probably the best choice. Here, when the searing heat of midday has passed, you can enjoy the late afternoon and the pleasant warmth of the evening.

An inviting extension to the main house can be created quite simply and cheaply. Potted plants may be used to provide a living foliage screen for privacy as well as a decorative focus. Here the impressive yellow trumpet flowers of brugmansia brighten the cool shaded corner.

**Right** When choosing a site for a patio consider when you are most likely to use it, and for what purpose. One that gets the sun earlier in the day is probably the best choice if you propose to sit out in the late afternoon.

**Opposite** Black and white chequered paving unite the interior of the house with the patio and pergola beyond. Such continuity of design pleases the eye and effectively extends the house area into a spacious outdoor living room.

Shade and privacy on a patio can be achieved in a number of ways, none of which need be either expensive or permanent. An illusion of privacy, for example, can be created quite simply: large attractive containers with impressive sculptural plants – a Chinese fan palm (*Livistona chinensis*), a lady palm (*Rhapis excelsa*) or a Swiss cheese plant (*Monstera deliciosa*), with its decorative and arresting leaves – could form an exotic 'wall' of foliage. Alternatively, trellis or wattle fencing, supporting a vigorous, preferably deciduous, climber (such as *Vitis vinifera*, the grape vine) would give a greater feeling of seclusion.

Roofing over a least part of the patio will mean that its use extends to those days when the weather is less clement and that in the winter months it can be used to protect plants from overhead frost. However, if you decide to build a pergola, or to attach some other form of overhead shelter onto the house, bear in mind that it may cut down the light level indoors considerably. Moreover, any structure expected to support a mature climber needs to be strong enough to do so. You may need to take professional advice on this.

The best permanent roof cover is glass, but this is not only expensive, it is also unwieldy and extremely heavy and therefore needs a correspondingly strong supporting structure. Next best is polycarbonate sheeting. It comes in a variety of thicknesses, is very strong and lasts indefinitely.

Your choice of flooring materials will depend as much on your purse as on the effect you wish to achieve. Possible materials are described in the section on Paving (pages 30-33).

If the patio is to be used literally as an extension of the house, then access must obviously be easy. The larger the entrance or doorway, the better. Not only does this make through traffic easier and safer, it helps maintain continuity between the indoor and outdoor areas. This can be further emphasized by echoing the interior in the design of the patio – perhaps in details of colour, pattern or texture. Clearly you can use this area as a vehicle for self-expression every bit as much as any of the inside rooms of your house.

Plants grown in containers will enhance the patio setting, with the advantage that if space is needed they can be temporarily set aside. Advice on selecting suitable containers and caring for these plants is given on pages 48-49.

Finally, since you are almost certainly going to want to eat or entertain on the patio after dark, you must give some thought to lighting. The choice is enormous, but in order to comply with safety regulations, you must have any form of outdoor patio lighting professionally installed. As long as there is no marked difference in lighting intensity, the distinction between house and garden will be minimized and the illusion of an extra outdoor living room successfully maintained by night as well as day.

# DRY, LOW-MAINTENANCE GARDENS

Even those of us lucky enough to live in a hot, dry climate all our lives may not be able to devote as much time to the garden as we would wish. But there are many people who visit their holiday homes in Mediterranean regions only for short periods each year, and who do not necessarily want to employ someone to care for their garden while they are away. At the same time, however, they would like to have a neat and attractive area around their house. In the absence of the gardener, the critical task most likely to be neglected is that of watering. Fortunately, however, lack of water does not rule out the possibility of achieving an attractive garden.

After all, any wild site is a natural low-maintenance garden. The only gardeners on a Mediterranean hillside, for example, are sheep, the only fertilizer their droppings and the only irrigation the rain. But how many marvellous plants you find there: gnarled olives a thousand years old; deep green twisted carobs; almonds dropping their petals round their feet in early spring; cistus, brooms, asphodels, rosemary and thyme all surviving in the rough untended scrub.

So, if you have inherited a wild site, do no clearing at all until you are quite certain which of the plants already there can be used in your plans. Build your design around the pines, olives, pistachios, rhamnuses and phillyreas. Given a careful pruning and forming, generous treatment with a complete fertilizer and some weeding around the base, they will surprise you with their response. The more deformed and twisted the olives, carobs and holm oaks, the more character they will have when trimmed and fed. Bushes can be sheared into interesting rounded shapes. Paths can be threaded through wild groves. Do make sure, though, that paths are porous where they run round the dripline of trees (which is where the feeding roots are), and impervious elsewhere, so that nearby plants will benefit from the runoff when it rains.

Even if you do decide to conserve an original wild site in this manner, you will almost certainly want to augment the existing plants with cultivated garden varieties. And you may be tempted, if you have a good source of water, to think that you can supply their watering needs in your absence with an automatic watering system, such as one of those described on pages 142-45. Although this is theoretically possible, in my experience in the Mediterranean region it is almost impossible to create a foolproof watering system that will function effectively and water your garden unsupervised for more than a week at a time. Failures in the electricity supply upset the controllers, stray animals disturb the microtubes and, if you have overhead watering that does function efficiently during your absence, you will return to a major weed problem.

Unless you can find someone who will come in once a fortnight to give a thorough soaking to all the trees and shrubs, you should choose only those plants that will withstand the critical summer months when conditions become desertlike. Cacti, succulents and many of the palms are well-adapted to drought; other plants that will put up with very little water are indicated in the lists at the end of the book as well as in the main catalogue of plants beginning on page 54. Here such plants are coded with the letter 'd' for dry.

Conserve as much moisture as you can by planting tall trees, such as the Italian cypress (*Cupressus sempervirens*). Not only will the garden be protected from drying winds, the trees' shade will keep the summer temperature down and reduce evaporation. The Italian cypress is ideal for this purpose: it is narrow and tall, so it casts a long shadow, and it does not have hungry roots, so you can garden beneath it.

Windbreaks are effective downwind for a distance of something like ten times their height, and are most efficient if they allow about 40 percent of the wind to filter through, thus avoiding turbulence. So plant your columnar cypresses 2.5 m/8 ft apart, to leave sufficient space between them when they are fully grown, or plant at half this distance and take out every other tree when they begin to grow too close together.

In a really dry garden a lawn is out of the question. It is therefore sensible to invest in large areas of good-quality paving or tiles – both better than gravel for keeping down weeds. These might be terraced on several levels if your site is sloping, and will provide attractive, trouble-free areas for strolling or sitting out. Although the initial outlay is high, the longterm practical advantages of such undemanding surfaces make

**Above** Undemanding yet arresting in its simplicity, this patio garden was designed around two existing olive trees. A wide variety of cacti provide a year-round display.

**Overleaf** 'Any wild site is a natural low-maintenance garden.' Bearded irises, gladioli and pelargoniums add colour and charm, fitting perfectly into this 'natural' terraced setting.

them a sound investment.

Low-maintenance, low-growing shrubs used as ground cover are the solution favoured by many. Many attractive herbs and shrubs, including ivies, are available that will cloak the soil, choke out the competition – and save the gardener work. In the section on Lawns and Ground Cover (pages 34-36) you will find suggestions that will provide good cover as well as, in some cases, a welcome splash of colour at certain times of the year.

All ground-cover plants require a degree of watering, weeding and periodic cutting – not to mention fertilizing and the occasional replanting of spots that have died off. They are still relatively undemanding, though, and make an effective, softer and more natural-looking alternative to large expanses of paving.

# TERRACED HILLSIDE GARDENS

As a trick for cultivating hillsides, terracing is almost as old as cultivation itself, and many houses on the Mediterranean littoral, as well as in some parts of California, for example, will have at least part of a stepped terrace on their land.

When investigating the site belonging to your house, you may come across a crumbled section of terracing; it is well worth considering having it restored and incorporated into the design of your garden. In the Mediterranean region of the Old World, such a section is likely to have been built originally with drystone walls. While these look attractive and have great character, they do have an annoying tendency to collapse and demand a lot of maintenance. Hints on how to deal with this when it happens, as well as on how to prevent it happening in the first place, are given on pages 37-38.

If your garden is on a hillside and you do not have a terraced area, it is well worth considering the merits of terracing at least part of the site. Though this could appear a prohibitively expensive proposition, bear in mind how much greater use you will get from the site as well as the broader range of gardening possibilities it will open up.

Broad terraces with low retaining walls, linked by broad flights of shallow steps or by paths, can be used to great advantage. Not only do they make maximum use of space, they create an impressive feeling of spaciousness in the garden.

Where terracing catches the sun for most of the day, consider planting the level nearest the house with large,

Lush and exuberant planting in this terraced hillside garden offsets the architectural simplicity of the house. Every design opportunity has been seized, from the splendid cycad that provides a fine centrepiece on the upper terrace to the thick brilliant carpet of bougainvillea below. Additional, softening, colour masses are provided by the plantings on the terrace walls themselves.

The taming of a difficult terrain has been achieved particularly successfully in both these terraced sites, one in California (above) and the other in the South of France (right).

Ease of maintenance is clearly a priority on any steeply terraced site. A few container-grown flowering plants and, of course, the lawn, are all that require watering.

In the French garden planting is similarly restricted to undemanding subjects. The impressive vertical masses of the cypress spires provide a dramatic backdrop.

Low box hedges and gravel paths have a restrained 'classical' formality and ordered simplicity that contrast with the wild beauty of the surrounding countryside.

broad-leaved deciduous trees, such as the plane (*Platanus* × *acerifolia*) or the drought-resistant *Celtis australis*. These trees will provide welcome shade to cool the house in summer, while in the winter the sun will shine through their bare branches to warm it, and the branches themselves will form an attractive tracery against the sky.

On lower terraces simple wooden pergolas can be erected to support sun-loving climbers that provide cool, shaded areas for walking or sitting. Plants that will do well in this role are discussed in the section on Pergolas on pages 38-41.

If a hillside of regular terracing seems to impose too rigid a discipline of horizontal lines, why not devote every other level principally to shrubs and trees. Line the paths on the terraces between with low-growing perennials. As you walk along, you will enjoy a novel bird's eye view of the trees and shrubs below, and your terraces will seem twice as wide. Another way of breaking up apparent rigidity is to build a wide flight of steps down the length of the terraces, so that each one opens off, right and left, as you descend.

Plants can be used to soften the hard lines of terraces. Terraces given over entirely to low-maintenance cacti and succulents can look dramatic and impressive. If you prefer more colour you can achieve it in raised beds or containers (pages 46-50), or in small beds flush with the walls from which cascades of flowers trail down to the terrace below. Ultimately your choice will depend on the availability of a water source.

# GARDENS WITH WATER

The gleam of water adds a new and vital dimension to any garden setting. Whether in ornamental ponds or pools, fountains or cascades, the sight and sound of water provide welcome relief from the aridity of long hot summers. Even a full-sized swimming pool can be made an attractive feature if it is designed in such a way that it blends with the existing garden landscape.

Again we can turn for inspiration to the Moors, past masters in creating refreshing oases in places where the summer drought is severe. Their great gardens in southern Spain display the art of using water in all its splendid variety. The great Italian gardens, too, incorporated quite spectacular water effects – the famous fountains of the Villa d'Este being but one example.

This way of using water is only possible with an abundant water supply and extremely sophisticated and powerful systems. Cataracts, waterfalls, runnels of rushing water, high plumed fountains – all are intended to astound, to excite and impress by the sheer volume of water, the noise and bravura of the special effects. Such 'Niagaras', however, are appropriate only to the scale of an important house and large garden. In a smaller domestic context they would not only be unsuitable, they would probably be unwelcome. Any noisy water effects are best restricted to areas where activity is always taking place – in the entrance area to the house or beside a flight of steps, for example.

In a small space water can be used to introduce gentle movement and interest – in an area enclosed by high evergreen hedges, for example, which might otherwise seem rather static and oppressive. In a secluded courtyard or a quiet corner of a patio, a small spout of water or a trickle from a bowl into a pond will also add a new and appealing dimension of sound.

Used as a mirror to reflect architecture or statuary – immobile elements – water can induce a feeling of calm. Since even a ripple on the surface would shatter the reflection and the sense of peace, water used in this way is best reserved for sheltered courtyards. In the Court of Myrtles at the Alhambra, planting is formal and restricted to well-trained orange trees and myrtle hedges. In other situations, the ever changing patterns of moving foliage reflected in the water may be entirely acceptable and desirable.

An attractive alternative to a small pond is a bog garden (page 44).

The imaginative use of water will transform any garden setting. Even the most modest of pools – no more than a few centimetres deep – will introduce a quality at once refreshing and relaxing.

**Right** Water mirrors the beauty of the surrounding trees and flowers, doubling the delights of this secluded corner. All depends on the stillness of the composition that reflects the stately *Strelitzia reginae* and the common flag iris.

Water may also reflect the patterns of delicate overhead foliage dancing in the breeze.

**Opposite** A successful synthesis of the practical and the aesthetic, this swimming pool in a Californian garden blends perfectly with its surroundings. Far from being intrusive, the blue introduces a jewel-like brightness in the verdant setting. Skilfully integrated into the garden design, a pool can become an ornamental feature in itself.

## SWIMMING POOLS

Considerable ingenuity and design skills are needed to find ways of making most swimming pools fit unobtrusively into the surrounding landscape. Gleaming stainless steel ladders, the brilliant blue of the water, the shouts of bathers, the whirr of pumps and the smell of chlorine are quite out of keeping with the natural sights and fragrances of the well-composed garden.

Though it is perfectly possible to construct pools that look more 'natural' by, say, making them an irregular shape, perhaps siting them under a rock, and lining them with more natural-coloured tiles – most people still seem to prefer the sanitized hygienic look. They would rather bathe in a clear bright blue pool than one that looks as though crocodiles might lurk in it.

The planting round a pool can help soften its 'clinical' appearance. Grass makes a perfect surround. Not only does it help reduce the artificiality of the pool itself, it is soft to walk or lie on, water drains quickly through it, and it does not get slippery, either with water or with suntan oil. Do not bring grass too close to the edge, however: heavy foot traffic too close to the water and the hosing down area may result in its becoming unpleasantly muddy. The thick thatch of St Augustine grass, described on page 34, is best suited to this purpose. It is essential that the area immediately around

the pool itself should be nonslip and easy to clean.

Farther from the water's edge, two main considerations apply to the choice of plants. The first seems obvious but is surprisingly often disregarded: none of the planting should be of a kind liable to damage bare flesh. Plants with hard spikes, such as the agaves, many of the yuccas, and a number of aloes – as well as young palm trees whose horrific spines at the leafbases can cause festering wounds – are all extremely dangerous. Be careful, too, not to plant anything near a pool that is likely to attract bees. Neither, of course, do you want trees or shrubs which might shed spent flowers, leaves or bark that might foul up the pool or its filters. Instead use foliage plants such as *Fatsia japonica, Schefflera arboricola*, and *Strelitzia nicolai*.

One attractive solution is to plant the margin with trees that not only provide shade but also impart a 'tropical' island look, in keeping with the blue waters. Mature palms, cordylines and bananas are all satisfactory and give precisely the desired impression. With the first two, however, you may wish to remove the flower spikes so that they do not shed petals. The leaves either fall entire and are easily removed (as in the case of the phoenix palm) or they remain as a shag around the trunk (as in Washingtonia). The shag can be left or removed periodically by an expert.

# ELEMENTS OF DESIGN

Mediterranean gardens tend, in general, to have a rather 'hard' feel compared to those in regions where there is less need to conserve water. Since lawns are only really satisfactory if they are watered in hot weather, paving of one form or another is often used to surface at least part of the garden.

Stone, for patios, paths and steps, and gravel, for walks, play a major part in their design. Walls, clipped hedges and pergolas are needed for protection from drying winds and to give shade and privacy. The sight and sound of water – so precious in hot dry climates – is often added in the form of ornamental ponds and small fountains.

This 'architectural' approach has its compensations. The soft areas of your garden, the flower beds and lawns, are reduced in area – with a corresponding reduction in weeding and maintenance. And though the laying of paving, the planting of hedges, or the building of terraces is always an expensive business, such gardens may prove economical in the long run. You will, for example, need to purchase few annuals to achieve a colourful display: their impact, framed by an area of contrasting grey stone, or surrounded by cobbles, will be even greater than in the midst of a border.

# PAVING AND
# HARD SURFACES

There are so many different materials available, offering such a wide range of textures and patterns, that you can make the hard surfaces an important decorative element in your overall garden design.

The cheapest hard surface is concrete; its hard grey appearance can be much improved and softened to a more natural tone by dusting over the wet surface with brown cement, or even soil, mixing it in slightly with a straw brush. Its rather forbidding appearance can also be much improved by breaking up a barren expanse of concrete with strips or squares of cobbles.

On large ornamental areas with little foot traffic, cobbles intersected with cut stone blocks can look very handsome. Variations on this theme were widely used by the Moors in southern Spain, who made elaborate patterns with different orientations of 'flat' cobbles of various colours laid on edge.

A surface of concrete patterned with cobbles is not only attractive, but easy and quick to make. The advantage of using cement as the base is that you prevent the paving from becoming infested with weeds. You should let the cobbles into the surface of the concrete bed as soon as it has been laid, before it has time to dry. Flat pebbles, about 80mm/3in in diameter are ideal, but it does not matter if the stones are not perfectly smooth – so long as they have one more or less smooth surface uppermost.

Set the stones at 100-150mm/4-6in centres, with the flattest side uppermost and flush with the surface of the concrete. Just as the concrete sets, wash and brush the pebbles to remove any traces of cement.

If you wish to make a pattern of alternating strips or squares of pebbles and concrete, lay the concrete first. Set out formers of planks, and pour the cement into them. Once this has set hard, you can lay the pebbles. Use a flat edge resting on the cast areas on either side to check that you lay them to the correct depth.

In order to soften the effect of a large expanse of paving, leave some gaps and plant them with ground-cover species such as creeping thyme, a fragrant herb that does not object to being walked upon.

Since paving is expensive you might consider economizing in certain areas by laying limestone chips, crushed stone or gravel instead. This could provide an effective and attractive contrast to large flat areas of stone. Although these chips make an ideal freely draining surface for pots and containers, they are not suitable for frequent traffic.

Cheap unglazed tiles look well around the house and help to provide that continuity between indoors and outdoors that is such an attractive feature of garden design in warm countries. Since such tiles are rather thin, they should be set in a concrete base if they are to withstand regular use.

Bricks set in sand make good paving around trees, where you want rain to filter through to the roots. Another way of dealing with those underused spaces under specimen trees – and one that does not harm their roots – is to build a raised wooden deck around the bole. If you make this some 2m/6ft across and about 300mm/12in high, you could throw cushions on it and use it as a sitting or reclining area, perhaps close to your barbecue.

Decks or wooden terraces around houses, often built up over rocky slopes, are particularly popular in the United States. Redwood, teak, or cedar are the only timbers that do not need regular treating with preservative, but since these are not readily available in the Mediterranean region itself, decking as a design solution is less popular there. To prevent the surface of a wooden deck becoming slippery, scrub it down in spring and autumn with salt or a proprietary cleaner, roughing it up with a wire brush and then hosing it down.

The same reservations would apply to the use of wooden blocks for paving in areas where good, dense hardwoods are not readily available. One possible alternative, for use in this situation, would be the wood of *Cupressus sempervirens* or Italian cypress, provided that it has been thoroughly soaked in a preservative.

When laying any surface, incorporate lengths of ceramic or plastic drainage pipes below the surface at regular intervals. Later, if you want to lay an irrigation system round the garden (see pages 142-46) or pass an electric cable for lighting under the path, instead of having to cut channels through the surface you can simply push the hose or cable through the pipes, thereby saving expense and disruption.

**Above** The colour and texture of materials chosen for hard surfaces establishes the character of a patio, courtyard or terrace. Here brick paving creates an informal relaxed impression.

**Left** Old stone steps, gravel paths and shady foliage contribute to the timeless appeal of this porch. Using local materials that are appropriate in a particular setting will always give pleasing results.

**Opposite page** Water-worn flat pebbles are laid on edge in a variety of directions and patterns. Although visually attractive, this kind of surface is not particularly comfortable to walk on.

**Left** Bricks, tiles and cobbles can make attractive and labour-saving surfaces. Flat pebbles can be laid on edge, perhaps, as here, in flowing *fleur-de-lys* and lozenges within a border of darker stones.

# LAWNS AND GROUND COVER

Despite all that has been said about the advantages of hard surfaces, it has to be admitted that a good lawn is an attractive garden feature, even – or perhaps especially – in a hot dry climate, where an expanse of green turf makes a strong and refreshing contrast to the parched ochre hues of the rest of the summer countryside.

Unfortunately, it is almost impossible to create a lawn that looks natural and beautiful for the whole year round. Either you choose a tropical grass which is adapted to the heat and drought and looks green and healthy in summer – and brown and dead in winter; or you go for a grass adapted to temperate climates, which will look good in winter – and miserable in summer.

## GRASSES FOR SUMMER LAWNS

The two best grasses for summer lawns are tropical in origin and well adapted to heat and drought.

St Augustine grass (*Stenotaphrum secundatum*) is a broad-leaved grass that spreads by runners and quickly makes a thick, springy mat. Some people do not like its coarse appearance, but there are now several improved strains with smaller and more delicate leaves. It is probably the most trouble-free summer ground cover: it needs little watering and the runners are fairly easily pulled up if they spread to parts of the garden where they are not wanted. It also grows well near the sea.

To establish this grass, take lengths of stem about 150mm/6in long and half bury the basal end of each one on a bed of prepared earth at a distance of about 250-300mm/10-12in from its neighbour.

The best time to plant St Augustine grass is early summer. Conditions are too cold for it to 'take' before that and the later you leave it the less chance you have of achieving a good lawn by the end of the summer. You can still plant up to the beginning of autumn, but you will not then get a good lawn until the following year.

Bermuda grass (*Cynodon dactylon*) is a creeping, fine-leaved grass that, with only moderate watering, looks green and healthy in summer, and makes beautiful smooth, professional-looking turf. If, in the hottest part of summer, water runs low, you can leave it dry. It will soon become brown, but even in this state it forms quite a pleasant ground cover, and at the first shower or watering it will quickly flush into green growth again.

Since it grows quickly from seed (which is not too expensive) and soon starts to send out runners, you can establish a good turf in a short time once the weather warms up. The propensity to run may well cause difficulty at the edges of beds, but problems can be kept to a minimum by laying stone or concrete slabs along the margin between the border and the lawn.

*Dichondra micrantha* is a low dense creeping plant that is not in fact a grass but is often used to make a lawn in the United States. The tiny bright green rounded leaves look attractive on their own or mixed with Bermuda grass. It does not turn brown in winter and tolerates some shade, but it does not wear well under heavy foot traffic and needs to be nourished and kept fairly moist. If you mix it with Bermuda grass you will have to use your judgment about when and how to mow: you will benefit dichondra by mowing high and seldom, the Bermuda grass by mowing close and often.

You cannot do much to keep a tropical grass lawn

**Opposite** Ground cover laid in patterns: lozenge-shaped 'beds' of *Lysimachia nummularia* 'Aurea' make a dense carpet of yellow foliage that contrasts with the dark green of the surrounding grass.

**Above** Low-growing aromatic plants, such as lavender, rosemary and grey leaved santolinas, make attractive ground covers. Here a seemingly flat expanse, planted principally with lavender, is broken up by pyramids of box and elegant urns.

green in winter, when it turns brown because of the cold, except dye it. Improbable as this may sound, it is common practice in the United States, and suitable dyes are becoming readily available elsewhere. On the other hand, you can keep a temperate grass green in summer by heavy watering at two- or three-day intervals. If you have a small lawn and an abundant supply of water this is a viable solution. Another option is to over-seed a lawn made of tropical grass with a fast-growing species – such as annual rye grass (*Lolium multiflorum*) – in autumn, so that as the green fades from one grass it is replaced by the other.

## GROUND COVERS

Alternatively, you can give up on grasses altogether, and use other ground-cover plants instead. Of the half-dozen or so most useful ground-cover plants, the most versatile is ivy. In its more vigorous forms ivy makes a thick, debris-swallowing, drought- and shade-resistant carpet. Its only disadvantage is that, left to itself, it climbs up and smothers everything it encounters.

The best of the more vigorous forms are as decorative as they are useful and may be used as climbers as well as ground cover. *Hedera colchica* has dark, leathery heart-shaped leaves, and its cultivar 'Dentata Variegata' is so heavily variegated that its leaves are often more creamy than green. *H. canariensis* has similar wide leaves on reddish stems, and its cultivar 'Gloire de Marengo' has creamy-white borders.

Lavender makes an excellent and fragrant ground cover though, of course, its colour and scent do not last year round. Choose either *Lavandula dentata*, an evergreen with an attractive ragged-edged leaf, or *L.* 'Grappenhall', with long, narrow leaves.

For an equally interesting colour effect, you might try *Lysimachia nummularia* 'Aurea'. This makes a pretty mat of roundish leaves, yellow at first but turning yellow-green with age. Planted in shade the leaves will be green.

Another particularly good ground cover, which also doubles for walls, is *Trachelospermum jasminoides*, the star jasmine. It is dense and evergreen, with very fragrant flowers, and will grow in full sun or light shade.

Any of the many forms of *Ajuga reptans* are also excellent in sunny or lightly shaded areas, provided that they are watered every ten days or so. The bronze cultivars, such as 'Atropurpurea' or 'Burgundy Glow', show a strong contrast to the silver-grey leaves of *Santolina chamaecyparissus*, another good cover. Also silver-grey are the trailing gazanias, which have the added benefit of brilliant yellow or orange flowers. *Erigeron karvinskianus*, a plant that looks like a graceful, fragile and small-flowered daisy, but which has the constitution of a donkey, is another excellent ground cover.

A lush expanse of green turf may provide an attractive contrast in the height of summer with the parched tones of the surrounding countryside. Choose a grass that is well adapted to heat and drought and be prepared to water it regularly.

# WALLS, HEDGES AND PERGOLAS

As well as offering protection from the elements, screens, whether natural or prefabricated, can be used to enclose the garden both vertically and horizontally, and to define axes and vistas. They give the garden form and, by concealing parts of it, make it more interesting, imparting an air of mystery and inviting exploration. On a slope they may be used to give a feeling of stability.

Pergolas, walls and hedges all provide microclimates due to the shade they cast, the protection they give from the wind and, in the case of south-facing walls, the heat they give off as infrared radiation. Choose plants to fit these conditions. Plant cacti, for example, along the foot of a south-facing garden wall with snapdragons and foxgloves on the other side of it.

## WALLS

Walls have certain advantages over hedges. They are built quickly and do not change their height or width with age. Since they have no roots, they do not interfere with the growth of plants at their foot and you can grow plants up them. Neither do they suffer from disease. In sum, you trade a high initial cost for low maintenance.

Building drystone walls is a skill no longer possessed by many people. If you can afford the expense of having a terrace built in this way, make sure that the wall is concave or flat, with a distinct lean towards the hillside. It should be backed by stones of various sizes, stretching 1m/3ft into the terrace to provide drainage. The base should be built of the largest stones, with a steady gradation in size from the bottom to the top. The wall should be finished with a capping of large stones.

If a wall falls down, there is little you can do but rebuild it. One cause for collapse is the alternate soaking and drying out of the earth behind it. The resulting contraction and expansion slowly pushes a belly of soil into the wall which eventually bursts.

The answer is to rebuild it on a firm base of large stones, and to improve the drainage. If the terrace continues to collapse, you will have to consider additional measures to strengthen it.

Brick walls with recessed arches and brick floors constitute the principal design feature in this Californian garden. Walls require little maintenance; they can be used, as here, to support climbers, and they provide sheltered microclimates that may favour particular plants.

If you are starting from scratch, you can 'cheat' a little by building a wall of building blocks and running reinforcement rods down the cavities which you then fill with cement. Leave gaps every half metre (twenty inches or so) along the bottom for drainage. A little way short of the top, run a couple more rods along the wall horizontally to tie it on either side. If you then face the wall with dry stones you will have a structure that is indistinguishable from the 'real thing', but stronger – and you should have no further trouble.

## HEDGES

Not only do hedges have a more natural feel, they serve as a refuge and resting place for birds. But while hedges are comparatively cheap and easy to start, slow-growing species, such as box, may take ten years to reach a reasonable height while fast-growing ones may need trimming several times a year. Most need watering and some need periodical spraying with insecticides.

Take care when planting a hedge along the edge of a terrace. If this has been properly made, the carefully fitted large blocks that form the face will be backed by as much as 1m/3ft of loose stones. Do not plant within 1.5m/5ft of the edge of the terrace, at the very minimum, in order to avoid this band of stones. Moreover,

cutting the top of a hedge along a terrace will be much easier if you can lean the ladder on the outside of the hedge with its feet on the top of the wall. Hedges should always be cut with a face that slopes inwards towards the top, to prevent the base dying and, on terrace edges, to avoid them overhanging the wall at the base in an ungainly fashion.

## PERGOLAS

A pergola is usually a wooden archway or framework over which to train shade-providing climbing plants. It can be either a freestanding structure that provides an attractive focal point in the garden or attached to the house itself. The Latin word *pergula* means a projecting roof, or eave, and the house walls can be used as part of the support for the horizontal struts. Both the upright and the horizontal struts can be made of wooden poles, old roof beams, galvanized angle iron or even, so far as the uprights are concerned, cement irrigation tubes filled with reinforcement rods and cement. Metal poles should not be used because the heat they absorb from the sun will scorch the plants that you try to grow up them.

Pergolas can be roofed with a semi-permanent material such as wooden slats, which will last many years if

**Left** Drystone walls look beautiful but may require a lot of maintenance. If you are building one from scratch, you can cheat a little by facing a more robust structure with dry stones.

**Opposite** Hedges contribute to the garden's architectural framework, and make an excellent foil for planting schemes and hard surfaces.

The Italian cypress, probably the best known and most typical Mediterranean tree, is immensely versatile and can be used in a wide variety of situations.

**Top left** Clipped *Cupressus sempervirens* – the Italian cypress – provides a permanently

green backdrop to the seasonal colour of pink osteospermums.

**Top right** Box-edged beds line a gravel path that leads to the garden's focal point: a silver obelisk set against a carefully shaped hedge of *Cupressus sempervirens*.

**Below left** Tall trees provide not only shade but an effective windbreak. Precious moisture is conserved since less is lost through evaporation in drying winds.

**Below right** Straight lines of clipped box provide both basic structure and ornament in every season.

**Above** Deciduous climbers, such as the wisteria clothing this impressive pergola, provide much-needed shade in summer but allow sunshine through to warm the inside of the house in winter.

**Right** Gnarled branches of wisteria twine around the elegant stone columns that support this ancient pergola. The delicate racemes of mauve blossoms that adorn it in early summer add yet another dimension to its beauty.

**Far right** Pergolas, like patios, can make an attractive visual link between house and garden. This one has an elegant simplicity that makes it a design feature in its own right. It looks good in winter as well as in summer.

painted annually with a half and half mixture of cheap olive oil and diesel fuel. Split bamboo roofing will last little more than a summer if, as is usual in the Mediterranean region, it is made of *Arundo donax* canes. Pergola roofs look best, however, when covered by trained plants. Indeed pergolas may have been developed by early gardeners specifically for the cultivation of grape vines, and vines are still among the best coverings for open screens. Vines that produce good table grapes have an additional appeal, but they will need a certain amount of care if you want them to produce good fruit.

As an alternative, you could try *Actinidia deliciosa* (syn. *A. chinensis*), the climber that produces the kiwi fruit. But you need a large, strong pergola for this plant which is very vigorous and bears a great weight of foliage. For successful fruiting you need to grow at least two plants – one male and one female.

Wisterias, with their long pendulous clusters of fragrant flowers, also look lovely draped over a pergola; their only disadvantage is that they take some time to get going and need pruning to flower well.

The advantage of these deciduous climbers – as noted earlier - is that they provide shade in summer but do not block the light in winter. If you prefer a semi-evergreen effect, the passion flower (*Passiflora caerulea*) or *Jasminum polyanthum*, with its highly fragrant blooms, are both attractive and vigorous. Roses, of course, are the traditional covering for pergolas, and rambling roses in particular are favoured for their semi-permanent pliable stems that make them easy to train. The hybrids of *Rosa wichuraiana*, and the cultivars of *R. banksiae*, or *Rosa* × *fortuneana* are especially useful as they are more or less evergreen in mild winter climates.

An excellent screen, incidentally, can be made by erecting lengths of chain link fencing (of as large a mesh as you can find) and allowing ivy to cover it. It matters little how ugly the support is. It will quickly be covered in green, glossy foliage.

Remember, though, that many plants used to cover pergolas have evolved their climbing habit in order to seek the sun – growing up beyond the shade cast by competitors. Because of this their stems are often bare, and the sides of your pergolas may need planting with low-growing shrubs for complete cover.

# WATER FEATURES

Even the smallest backyard or balcony can benefit from the imaginative use of water and there are numerous ways in which this element can be introduced. Ponds need be no more than several centimetres (a few inches) deep. Most, however, will require professional help with their design and construction. The qualities water contributes to its setting are manifold: it offers both aural and visual delight. Your enjoyment of it, however, will be marred if its purity and clarity are sullied. There are a number of precautions and remedies you can put into effect in order to keep it crystal clear.

## WATER CARE

One of the problems with ornamental ponds in places with very hot climates and chalky water is that the water evaporates in the heat and leaves behind a surface scum of calcium carbonate (chalk). In a pool with a fountain

**Above** Choose waterlilies for the colour or fragrance of their blooms and the aesthetic shapes of their leaves. Among the most beautiful of all garden flowers, they do best in still water and full sun.

**Right** An enchanting setting framed by a keyhole arch demonstrates the skilful and imaginative use of water. Cascades of vibrant pink bougainvillea hover over still white waterlilies.

or other surface agitation, this scum will sink to the bottom. In a still pool, however, it will sit on the surface, taking away all its reflecting power. Flies and dust that fall on the surface also make the pool look cloudy. To avoid this it is worth installing a skimmer system as in a swimming pool.

Any pond or pool fitted with a circulating pump benefits from the installation of a biological filter. A network of small diameter rigid pipes, with a series of small holes drilled in their underside, forms the intake of the pump, the output being returned to the pond via a fountain or pipe. This 'tree' is laid on the bottom of the pond and covered in a 150mm/6in-layer of stone chips. After a month or so, the chips become 'active' through colonization by bacteria and algae and your pond water should become crystal clear.

All water gardens attract breeding insects. Some, like the dragonfly are ornamental, whereas others, such as the mosquito are noxious. Although dragonfly larvae are predatory (and may eat baby goldfish), the adults will give much pleasure with the spendid coloration of their bodies and their rapid aerial manoeuvrings.

Mosquito larvae in ponds are easily dealt with by introducing mosquito fish. These small brown fish are never more than 50mm/2in in length, even when fully developed, but they are fecund and tough and voracious feeders on the eggs, larvae and pupae of mosquitoes. Goldfish, too, will feed on mosquito larvae, but they breed less exuberantly and therefore correct an infestation more slowly. Unfortunately, mosquito fish have a taste for the eggs and fry of goldfish.

## RAISED POOLS

These are best excavated and constructed with professional help. It is not difficult to build a raised pool that will enable you to admire the appearance and enjoy the fragrance of water plants and to feed your Koi carp by hand without stooping too much.

If the pond is to bear the weight of the water without cracking, the slab of concrete that forms the floor must be at least 150mm/6in thick and strengthened with reinforcement rods. These should turn up into the building blocks, filled with concrete, that form the walls. A further series of rods should be placed in a ring one course from the top of the walls to prevent the walls from being pushed outwards.

Extreme care must be taken when setting up pumps or lights in pools. Strict regulations control the installation of outdoor electrical fittings in most countries: a trained contractor should be able to advise you. The system must be fitted with a differential circuit breaker that cuts off the power if contact is made with a live wire.

## WATER PLANTS

For me, one of the main reasons for having a pool is to grow waterlilies, which must be among nature's most beautiful plants. They produce exquisite flowers from early spring to autumn and their leaves make an attractive pattern in the water. Some varieties are also blessed with a strong fragrance.

Remember, though, that water effects and waterlilies are incompatible. Waterlilies are plants of still water and will not prosper if water from a fountain is continually splashing on their leaves or if the surface of the water is always agitated. To do well, waterlilies also need full sun.

One of the few disadvantages of waterlilies is that the leaves suffer from blackfly infestation in summer. The only way to get rid of them is to kill them with insecticide, choosing one that is not harmful to fish or other water life and spraying only the leaves, not the surface of the pond.

Lilies can be fed through the leaves, by spraying them with small quantities of dilute liquid fertilizer. Never use fertilizer, however, in the soil in which you plant the lily roots. Instead, the young tubers should be buried in plain garden soil, in a shallow pot or bowl, and sunk into the pond. You can give the plants a new lease of life every two or three years by lifting them, cutting off and replanting 150mm/6in-lengths from the growing points on the tubers and discarding the old wood and roots.

The lotus (*Nelumbo nucifera*), another beautiful water plant, has big round leaves and huge single pale pink flowers, both standing up above the surface of the water. It seems, however, to prefer slightly acidic water and you may have problems growing it in areas with highly alkaline soils. Iron chelate will help if added to the point where it hardly colours the water, and in this quantity seems to have no harmful effect on any fish.

## BOG GARDENS

Most gardeners imagine that the summer heat will quickly turn a wet spot into a dry, hard pancake of cracked mud but, in fact, the moisture loss is no greater than that from a pond. A bog garden is not difficult to make. Scrape the soil down to a depth of 300mm/12in from an area perhaps 1m/3ft wide and 4m/13ft long, and of any shape you like. Then cast a slab of cement

**Right** A pond carefully sited for quiet contemplation will give pleasure only as long as its water remains clear. Skimmer systems, pumps and filters help maintain clarity.

**Opposite** Raised ponds introduce an interesting and unusual dimension to any garden. Water from ponds can be ducted to adjacent bog gardens where a wide variety of moisture-loving plants will flourish.

The pond floor should be at least 150mm/6in thick and the walls strengthened with reinforcement rods to bear the weight of the water without cracking.

over the scraped area with reinforcement rods turned up in to the walls, exactly as if you were making a raised pond, but fill it with earth. In one corner, partition off an area just big enough to take a ballcock and valve, linked to the water supply. Make holes in the partition, at floor level, and stuff them with wire netting. Fill the main bog with peaty earth. The ballcock should be set so that it keeps the water level in the partitioned area at a depth of 50mm/2in. Water then seeps through the holes so the earth is always wet but only waterlogged at the very bottom. In winter you can turn off the water supply and give the occasional watering by hose.

In the moist environment of a bog garden you can grow species whose lush foliage will surprise visitors and contrast with the aridity of the rest of the garden. Many ferns will thrive, putting out generous plumes of delicate green leaves. Zantedeschia, commonly known as the arum or calla lily, has showy trumpets of white or coloured flowers in summer; it can be partnered with feathery astilbes, and the graceful sedges, *Cyperus papyrus* and *C. involucratus* (syn. *C. alternifolius*). If you want more showy plants, try *Pontederia cordata*, the pickerel weed, which has blue flower spikes all summer, and the spectacular *Iris ensata* (syn. *I. kaempferi*) that you can grow from seed. The latter thrives if you add iron chelate to the water. Other plants that do well are the forget-me-nots (myosotis), musk (mimulus) and the hostas.

# CONTAINERS
# AND RAISED BEDS

If you think of your garden as a room or a series of rooms, enclosed by hedges or walls and floored with grass or paving, then the pots and containers are the furniture, which you can adjust to suit your taste and vary the colour scheme. For many flat-dwellers, with no garden other than a window sill, container-grown plants are literally part of the furnishings. The popularity of indoor pot plants in Mediterranean regions is revealed whenever it rains in summer, and the pavements suddenly produce a crop of pots brought out so that their occupants may be refreshed.

Container gardening is ideal for anyone whose garden consists of no more than a small balcony, patio or roof garden, and for anyone who has to suffer troublesome cementlike clay soils, or shallow soils overlying solid rock. As likely as not, the soil around a modern house will be laced with builder's rubble, plaster and cement; here, too, it is best to pave the surface and use pots and containers (perhaps planting bougainvillea against the house walls, as this climber does not mind dry, compacted ground so much).

## CARING FOR POT PLANTS

Tender plants raised in pots can be treated as migrants, spending the summer out of doors and coming into the house, or under some form of shelter, for the winter months. Any kind of overhead shelter will provide some protection from the radiation frosts that occur on clear nights and are often lethal to tender plants. The sides can be open to the elements, for it is the roof that blocks the infrared radiation and protects the plants. If you want to grow a large number of migrant plants you may decide to build a conservatory or roof a part of the house with glass. This is not hard to arrange, as you can buy glass roof tiles that can be used to replace some of the clay tiles and will not spoil the look of the house.

A number of plants that are normally grown indoors can also be treated as migrants and moved into a shady corner of the garden in summer: rubber plants, kentia and areca palms, rhoicissus vines and scheffleras, for example. Tropical plants such as the dieffenbachias, dracaenas and spathiphyllums can be brought into the garden for short periods. However, they must never be

**Right** A delightfully profligate use of pots with colourful pelargoniums, petunias, lobelia and heuchera enlivens this simple stone exterior. Pots are safely secured with rails and metal rings.

**Opposite** An antique fountain, imaginatively planted, becomes the focal point of this courtyard. Before planting direct in such a container, drainage would have to be provided by a hole, covered with a thick layer of gravel, in its floor.

exposed to direct sunlight, or brought abruptly from low light conditions indoors to the full intensity of the bright outdoors. In their natural habitat these plants are densely shaded by tree cover; move them, by stages, from the most deeply shaded corners of the garden into a better illuminated spot, and then return them to the conditions they like most.

The gardener has a much more intimate relationship with a container-grown plant than with one planted in the garden. The pot plant is more dependent on the grower and the grower is more aware of the plant and its needs. You can inspect a pot plant's roots and control its food and drink, giving it the ideal soil mix and its own watering programme. You can easily move pots around, to make a seasonal display and hide those that are past their peak, or to try out new combinations of form and colour.

Gardening in pots has many advantages, but there are some drawbacks. Overheating of the roots is a common reason why pot plants die or suffer a check to their growth in hot climates. Unlike leaves, roots have no stomatal pores, so they can't keep themselves cool by sweating and, since they tend to gather around the outside of the soil mass for better aeration, they suffer dreadfully from the heat. So use clay pots that keep cool by evaporation, or wooden containers that insulate the roots. Avoid black plastic pots: they will absorb the sun's heat.

Keep your pots and containers shaded if you can; put them close together to shade one another, or plunge them in a bigger container of gravel or peat. Burying pots in an insulating layer of gravel or peat also protects them from the cold.

## CHOOSING POTS

Soil mixtures for pots need to be lighter, better draining and more water-retentive than good garden soil. This means that the pot will weigh less and be more likely to be blown over. There is no completely satisfactory answer to this conundrum. Pots with a wide base are more stable, but it is important to keep the container in scale with the plant. A small cactus in a large pot will look as silly as a tall tree in a tiny tub. Subject to the difficult problem of stability, you should try to keep the forms in harmony. A tallish small tree looks best in a tall pot, a spreading shrub in a wide, low basin.

When you buy a clay pot, lift it with one hand and tap it with the knuckle of the other. It should ring: if it sounds dull or creaky, the fabric of the pot is flawed or badly baked. The baked clay should be of a uniform colour. Colour variation indicates uneven firing, which means that one side of the pot will be less strong than the other. If the pot is underfired, constant contact with damp soil will eventually make it crumble.

When you repot your plants, always move up to a pot just a little bigger than the last. It is easy to feel that the more room a plant has for expansion the more quickly it will grow, but in fact it will do better in a pot that is just big enough: this is because a plant in a restricted space develops more roots, which means more water uptake and better aeration.

It is a good plan to place a 'saucer' beneath each pot, to avoid damp patches on your floor or furniture, and to hold a little water on which the plant can draw. Glazed clay saucers are best; unglazed saucers will allow water to seep through, unless you take the precaution, before planting, of coating the inside with impermeable bituminous paint or a silicone.

Since a plant in a pot has a much smaller reserve of water than one in the ground, watering is a far more critical matter. As a general principle, it is best to water once the surface of the soil has become dry, but before the soil shrinks and leaves a gap down the side of the pot. Water until the soil is saturated and the excess

liquid trickles out of the soil into the saucer. If you leave it too late and the soil has already shrunk plunge the whole pot in water until the soil has expanded again to fill it. Otherwise the water will simply flow down the gap and be of no benefit to the plant.

Water-absorbing granules, that retain moisture three times longer than any soil or compost, can be a boon. They are not expensive, and a few grams per litre of soil will suffice. Mix them with the soil before planting up your containers.

As water evaporates salts tend to build up in a pot, so it is a good idea, once every couple of months or so, to move the container to a sink or terrace where it can drain freely without damaging anything; then give the soil a thorough soaking, so that the water runs away out of the bottom of the pot, carrying dissolved salts with it. If the pot is made of clay, water the outside as well, for this is where evaporation deposits much of the salts.

Since the soil mixture in a pot is, or should be, open, the nutrients tend to leach out of it quickly. Moreover, there is less soil and therefore a smaller reserve of nutrients in a pot than in the open ground.

So the rule is to fertilize little and often. Most com-mercially prepared proprietary powders or liquids are suitable, if the directions are carefully followed. Don't get carried away by the idea that the more food a plant receives the faster and better it will grow. Beyond a certain point, overfeeding may exacerbate the problem of salinity (many fertilizers are salts of one kind or another), and, also, the plant may be poisoned by an excess of metallic ions that in small quantity (as trace elements) are essential, but in surfeit are either directly damaging or inhibit the uptake of other elements.

RAISED BEDS

Raised beds may be thought of as a form of container – the main difference is that they are permanent fixtures. Like containers, they allow the soil mixture to be varied according to the needs of the individual plants. Raised beds, maybe at several different levels, are also useful for breaking the monotony of a large expanse of paving. They make gardening easier as you grow older, or simply tire of stooping.

The optimum height for a raised bed is 600mm/24in from the ground. The beds can be curved or rect-angular, free-standing or built against a bank or garden

**Left** The rounded sculptural leaves of ligularia are echoed not only by the swelling forms of the antique oil jars but in the curves of the arch, the step ends and the window.

**Right** Ivy-leaved and zonal pelargoniums are ideal plants for sunny positions. They can happily tolerate lack of water and produce a constant show of colour from early spring until late autumn.

Carefully pruned lemon trees thrive in 18th-century terracotta pots in this Sicilian rooftop garden. Not only does the lemon fruit add colour and ornament to the plant, the blossom has an intense, delightful fragrance.

A raised bed provides an anchor point for this superb display. The dense white fragrant mass of star jasmine (*Trachelospermum jasminoides*), makes a stunning backdrop to the rampant pink pelargoniums.

wall – but do not build them against a house wall or you will suffer from rising damp. Free-standing beds can be up to 2m/7ft wide, depending on your reach. If the beds are accessible only from one side they should not be more than 1.2m/4ft across; if they are any wider you will find it difficult to weed the areas farthest away.

So long as you have no trees with roots that can reach the beds, there is no need to pave under them. If there are greedy-rooted trees nearby, however, it is best to pave or cement the whole area, to prevent roots coming up into the beds from below. This will give you the opportunity to move the walls of the beds around and experiment before they are cemented in place, so that you can be sure to site them to your liking. If they are to stand on impermeable paving remember to leave wrist-sized holes at metre intervals along the bottom of the wall for drainage.

If you construct your beds of ordinary building blocks you can render them and possibly even paint them afterwards, either in white or a colour to match the walls of your house.

The bottom two-thirds of the beds can be filled with a mixture of broken stones of about fist size. The soft sandstones and limestones used as building materials are ideal, because they absorb and retain moisture. Indeed, they are better at retaining moisure than the soil itself, since the cracks and discontinuities serve to interrupt the capillary action that, in an unbroken column of earth, is continually drawing water to the surface, where it evaporates.

These stone beds, topped with a mixture of five parts of garden soil to one of peat, provide ideal conditions for growing scree and rock-face plants, such as thymes and cyclamens, which need perfect drainage, and are more effective brought closer to eye level. Or use raised beds for growing acid-loving plants, such as gardenias, in a mixture of peat, grape pressings, spent mushroom compost and perlite.

# CHOOSING PLANTS

One of the most enchanting qualities of a garden is that it never stays the same for a day. Throughout its existence the relationships between masses, colours and textures are continually changing, never repeating themselves; and, as with most kinds of growth, this is particularly so when the garden is young.

A design plan would, ideally, take into account the state of the garden at five-yearly intervals over the course of about three decades – particularly if it is going to incorporate large trees. Such a counsel of perfection is, however, beyond most of us unless we have considerable experience of how fast each variety will grow in the particular conditions of any given soil.

All of us can, however, adopt an intelligent and practical approach to designing with plants simply by, in the first instance, having a clear conception of the type of garden we wish to create. In terms of its underlying structure and the plants you wish to grow, there are three types of garden: the architectural garden, the colour garden and the collector's garden.

The architectural garden achieves its effect through the contrast of forms, the interplay of textures, the setting of axes and crossings and the contrast of vertical and horizontal features. Interest is concentrated on steps, paving, walls, water features and statuary. There may be little diversity in the planting, which is likely to be confined to evergreens – whether trees or shrubs – chosen for the sculptural contribution of their mass to the overall scheme. Other planting will be limited to those subjects that are the least demanding to grow – since the architectural garden should require minimal maintenance.

The colour garden is for people who want flowers in and around the house all the year and are primarily concerned with colour contrasts and relationships. They will base their design on the wide selection of annual bedding plants, flowering shrubs and colourful perennials readily available in most nurseries.

The third type of garden – the collector's – is likely to be the choice of an experienced gardener who enjoys something unusual and would rather grow a rare plant for interest than a common one for effect. This may involve creating special growing conditions and a considerable allocation of time – once established, rare plants may have their own particular demands.

The three kinds of garden are distinct and though the elements of one may be imported into another, you should start with a clear idea of which you wish to achieve, or you will fall into a design jumble between the three. In any case, if you are to create a garden that is going to satisfy both you and others permanently, start by planning the overall effect and the placing of masses before you begin to think about precisely which plants will compose those masses.

While the choice of plants to incorporate into your garden design is greater than it has ever been, most growers still concentrate on the ones that have traditionally proved successful in their particular region. Over the years these have been found to be suited to the

A classically simple garden on the Côte d'Azur achieves its effect with neat lawns, pebbled paths and restrained and thoughtful planting.

For year-round colour, most nurseries will be able to supply flowering shrubs and colourful perennials as well as the popular summer bedding plants. Here the grey-green of neatly clipped lavender and the dark green of the box hedges provide a permanent framework for changing seasonal displays.

local climate and soil conditions; they are easy and cheap to reproduce, resistant to pests and, all in all, the least demanding plants to grow. Among them you will find suitable plants for the low-maintenance architectural as well as the colour garden.

Even if local regulations permit the importation of plants from other countries, be wary of purchasing attractively packaged shrubs, for example, until you have established that they are indeed suited to growing in climates that enjoy hot dry summers. An enterprising

nursery may have imported plants to suit a diverse range of local conditions and not all of them will necessarily grow in your garden.

When attempting to grow specialist plants, you can minimize the risk of unpredictable behaviour, or outright failure, by selecting subjects from those regions of the world with a broadly similar climate to the one you are gardening in. Just as the flora of northern Europe and North America was greatly enriched in the nineteenth century by introductions from the Himalaya,

This Mediterranean garden in Western Australia is clearly the creation of an enthusiastic and knowledgeable gardener. The use of colour – in the brilliant red and yellow cannas – is discreet but dramatic.

southern Chile and Japan, so gardens in the Mediterranean regions of the world have benefited from a similar interchange of species.

Select any new plant with care. Check that it will survive the lowest temperatures you experience in your area and that it will be tolerant, if necessary, of wet winter conditions. Take note also, if you live by the sea, of the plant's resistance to the presence of salt in the air, water or soil. Whether your soil is acid or alkaline will also dictate which plants you can incorporate into your design. It may be that the only way you can supply the needs of plants with marked preferences – such as that of gardenias and camellias for acid soil – is to grow them with the right soil mix in containers.

In the following section, Plants for Mediterranean Gardens, you will find all the information you need in order to assess whether or not a particular subject is suited to the situation you have in mind. Lists of plants suited to a variety of special growing conditions can be found on pages 150-53.

# PLANTS FOR MEDITERRANEAN GARDENS

The following pages present an illustrated catalogue of some 300 flowers, trees and shrubs that
are suitable for growing in a garden that enjoys a
Mediterranean climate. It includes all those plants
that are commonly available in nurseries in
Mediterranean regions, as well as some that you
can easily grow from seed.

The catalogue is intended to be both practical
and inspirational. You can use it to help make
choices when visiting a nursery or to amplify
accounts given in suppliers' catalogues. You can
use it to decide, when designing a garden or preparing a planting plan, which plants will best suit
the situation you can offer and if they will achieve
the effect you want to create.

So that you can tell at a glance whether or not a
particular plant will suit your purpose, each one is
accompanied by abbreviated details of the size it
may eventually achieve, the lowest temperature it
will tolerate, how thirsty it is likely to be, how
quickly it will grow under normal conditions,
whether or not it is suitable for growing on the sea
coast and when it looks its best. These details are
given in an easily understood coded form that is
explained on pages 56-7..

# EXPLANATORY NOTE TO THE CODES

After the name of each plant in this 'catalogue', you will find coded details that will indicate at once whether or not that subject is suited to your purpose.

One example will serve as explanation:

**Strelitzia reginae**
H 1.2m/4ft  S 1m/3ft  −2C°/28°F  n s c l

H and S refer to Height and Spread. (R, with reference to climbing plants that also trail and spread, indicates Reach.) Temperatures indicate the lowest temperature that plants will survive
n Indicates watering needs (in this case normal)
s Indicates speed of growth (slow)
c Indicates it will tolerate a coastal situation
l Indicates it looks best in late winter.
A few words on each of these will further clarify their meaning.

## HEIGHT, SPREAD AND RANGE
Plant growth depends on so many variable factors that it is impossible to be absolutely precise about these dimensions. For example, *Beaucarnea recurvata* usually reaches a height of a metre (three feet) after ten years, but I have seen examples in California and Mexico that are over six metres tall. Which is the most useful figure for height in this case? A large, longlived tree, such as an oak, will not reach full adult size for several decades, whereas an annual will reach it in one. A well-fertilized plant growing in deep earth may grow twice as large as one growing in poor shallow soil.

It has clearly been necessary to exercise a degree of judgment when estimating the figures for height and spread, and the dimensions given are based on those the plant should reach at early maturity in a well-managed garden under average Mediterranean conditions.

## COLD RESISTANCE
The temperatures given are the lowest at which the plant will survive in the Mediterranean region. The figure should be treated with some caution, since a number of conditions may modify it by several degrees. The major variable is the degree of hardiness or woodiness that a plant has achieved before it is exposed to cold. Many plants that are half hardy in climates with relatively wet summers are much hardier in places that have hot dry summers, since the heat and aridity not only stop the plant putting out soft new growth but also harden up the existing wood. Species from the inner parts of a continent often show this characteristic; for example, species from the mid-South of the United States tend to be hardier than plants from coastal regions. You can help tender shrubs build up a resistance to winter cold by keeping them on the dry side and under-fed.

There is a difference too in the susceptibility of different parts of a plant to aerial frost: the flowers are most vulnerable, followed by the leaves, then the stems, and, finally, the roots. For this reason you should never give a plant up for dead simply because it has been cut back to the ground by frost; there is a chance that the roots will have survived and, in time, new growth may well emerge.

Winter temperatures can differ widely, even between places that are relatively close to one another. Increasing distance from the coast, a situation in the bottom of a valley where cold air collects, or on a shaded slope as opposed to one that gets a lot of sun are factors that make a big difference to minimum temperatures. Even within a single garden there will be localized hot and cold areas where the difference in average temperatures may be as much as 5°C/9°F, as between the shady and sunny sides of a wall, for example.

## WATERING NEEDS
The letter 'n' (normal) means that plants should receive a deep watering at least once a week in summer. It can be reduced in winter, as long as the subsoil is kept wet at all times.

The letter 'd' (dry) means that the plant will grow in the open ground without additional watering under average Mediterranean conditions. All these plants will need occasional watering, however, until they are established and in periods of abnormal drought.

The letter 'o' (occasional) means the plant must be given a thorough soaking twice monthly in summer and once a month in spring, as well as in autumn and winter if there is little or no rain.

The letter 'm' (moist) is used for plants that will die if they ever dry out completely and which need watering every two or three days in the height of summer.

The letter 'w' (wet) is used for those few bog plants and water plants that grow best in waterlogged soil. Some will grow well under moist conditions, but a pond or bog is more economical on water, losing less through evaporation than a well-drained soil that needs frequent watering.

Since water is a commodity in short supply in most Mediterranean climates, plants have been classified towards the dry side of the ideal if they will accept such conditions. Thus some rated 'o' will make an acceptable show watered in that way, but will make a much better one if treated as 'n'. It is most important to remember that container-grown plants will need more frequent watering.

How much water you want to give the garden fixes the plants you can use within narrow limits. There is a wide choice of subjects that need no supplementary watering at all and that will last out the dry months of summer without dying even if there is no rain. On the other hand, drought-resistant plants are usually less spectacular than those that need abundant watering. You will also find that moisture-loving plants flower in summer, when most people want a colourful garden display, whereas those plants that are capable of surviving the drought are likely to be at their best in spring or autumn.

## SPEED OF GROWTH

Most people are interested in seeing the results of their planning and labour as soon as possible; they want fast-growing plants or those that will make an immediate effect. Fortunately many plants do indeed grow fast in Mediterranean climates, given enough water and food, because of the long growing season and relatively brief winters.

The letter 'a' (average) means that the speed of growth is much as you would expect from a plant of its type and eventual size.

The letter 'f' (distinctly faster than average).

The letter 's' (distinctly slower than average).

An 'f' does not always imply that the plant will form a huge body of foliage in a short time. It may mean that it gets away quickly and makes a good show in a few months, even though on a reduced scale compared with a mature specimen. You should also bear in mind the curious fact that some plants grow better for some people than for others and that sometimes they dislike their site for no very obvious reason; they simply refuse to get moving.

## SUITABILITY FOR COASTAL CONDITIONS

The letter 'c' (coast) indicates plants that will grow well close to the sea. There is no rule about 'close'. On windy, exposed coasts, salt spray may be carried some considerable distance inland.

## SEASON OF GREATEST INTEREST

The final figure in the codes indicates the season of greatest effect – that is, when the flowers, fruit, leaves or a combination of all these are especially attractive. If there is no figure, it can be assumed that the plant is attractive year round.

The figure 1 denotes late winter.

2 denotes spring and early summer.

3 denotes high summer.

4 denotes autumn and early winter.

# TREES

In gardens all over the world, trees are valued for the beauty of their form and foliage and – sometimes – flowers. In hot, dry climates, they have an added importance as providers of shade. Though trees grown in hot, dry regions are unlikely to attain the stature of those in cooler or in tropical climates, nonetheless, as more or less permanent features, often supplying architectural bulk, they make a significant contribution to the garden setting.

The health and speed of growth of any tree depends to a great extent on the care taken in its planting. It is all too easy to take a trowel or spade, remove a core of soil the size of the pot the plant arrived in, and drop the young tree into the hole – like a cork into the neck of a bottle. Preparing a tree correctly for planting demands a lot more effort, and so does digging it a large, deep hole lined with a good earth mixture. The rewards for this effort will be great – but they will not be apparent until a couple of years later.

Before planting, cut back the top of the young tree so that it is in balance with the roots. This is particularly important for bare-root trees, where it greatly increases the chances of a successful take – remember that the roots of field-grown plants are unavoidably damaged and reduced in the lifting, so you cannot expect them to maintain and feed an unreduced head of leaves when spring arrives. In the case of trees supplied in containers, cutting back is less crucial, and generally a little trimming is all that will be needed.

When planting trees, the new soil surface should be level with the soil mark on the trunk. Build a wall or rampart of earth, 150mm/6in or so high, around the trunk, at a radius of about 600mm/24in (a little more or less depending on the size of the tree), to prevent the water running away when you irrigate in summer.

It is important to ensure that all young trees, but especially tall specimens such as palms and Italian cypresses, are securely held in place. Wind-rock has the effect of breaking off all the small roots that are just beginning to grow out of the rootball. It may be necessary to tether tall trees with guyropes.

Except for tender plants such as hibiscus, bougainvillea, citrus or lantana (which should all be planted in spring), container-grown trees and shrubs are best planted in early autumn, so that they have time to establish themselves while the ground is still warm. They will then get away faster in the following spring.

Quite a few drought-resistant trees survive because they put down a deep taproot. They should be planted when small – brachychiton and eucalyptus, for example, are best set in a permanent site when only 150mm/6in high – and, once planted, should not be moved.

---

**Abies pinsapo**
H 25m/82ft S 10m/33ft −9°C/16°F d s
In general, firs grow on cool high mountains; this species, the Spanish fir, is found growing wild only in a few restricted sites in the high Sierra Nevada of southern Spain. It makes an attractive accent tree planted among rocks and does best at some altitude. Although drought resistant, it will not be happy without an occasional soaking. *A.* × *insignis* is the hybrid of *A. pinsapo* crossed with *A. nordmanniana* and is similarly useful.

**Acacia**
The acacias or wattles are a group of spectacular flowering trees. There are many different species, mainly from Australia, and nearly as many hybrids.

All acacias grow well from seed. Pick the pealike seed pods once they have turned brown, extract the seeds and pour on boiling water; leave them to cool and sow those that have swollen.

**Acacia dealbata hybrids**
H 15m/50ft S 12m/40ft −7°C/19°F d f c l
The term mimosa is usually applied to this group (syn. *Racosperma dealbatum* hybrids). They are expensive since they have to be propagated by grafting, a technique practised by only a few specialist nurseries. Small differences show between the different hybrids, principally in the colour of the flower and in the degree of silvery-grey in the leaf.

Treat the saplings with great care during transport and planting for they are brittle and the graft union is not always as strong as one might wish. You must stake the sapling – supporting the top securely with a plastic

Pinus, arbutus (centre), olive (right) and *Cupressus arizonica* 'Fastigiata' (bottom right)

*Acacia dealbata* hybrid

collar so as not to damage the bark – for these trees come from areas of low rainfall and in wet winters tend to grow too fast for the strength of their trunks.

As well as keeping the sapling staked for several years the branches should be cut back by up to half every year for the first few years. You can do this while the tree is in flower and bring the cut branches into the house. At the same time you can form the sapling either into an upright tree shape or into a more rounded bush. All mimosas are evergreens of very rapid growth but with a correspondingly short life of some twenty to thirty years. On limestone they are apt to suffer chlorosis and need dosing every now and then with iron chelate. They need no watering except for a good soaking two or three times in the summer during the first few years.

### Acacia cyanophylla
H 6m/20ft  S 6m/20ft  −5°C/23°F  d f c 2

The orange wattle has orange-yellow flowers in early spring and is quick to grow from seed. Another acacia commonly found in nurseries, *A. retinodes*, has rather small unspectacular flowers. It is, however, hardier than the other acacias and good on limestone.

### Ailanthus altissima
H 20m/66ft  S 12m/40ft  −9°C/16°F  d f c 3

Whoever named this 'the tree of heaven' must have envisaged a very competitive paradise, for it is an invasive tree that will grow where few others will: in big cities, in poor shallow ground, beside the sea, even in dunes which it serves to stabilize. Despite its Latin name, it does not grow very high; examples over 20m/66ft are unusual. Even so, it is not recommended for small gardens as it invades by suckers and by seeds.

You should plant only female trees because the flowers of the males have an unpleasant smell. The maplelike seed pods of the female are ornamental. One cultivar, 'Erythrocarpa', has especially large and strongly coloured fruit trusses and there is plenty of scope for further varieties with attractive characteristics. If you wish to restrict the tree's growth, cut young plants down to the ground each winter, after the leaves have fallen, allowing only one shoot to develop the following spring – in good conditions this will reach a height of over 1.2m/6ft in a year and bear huge ornamental pinnate leaves.

## Albizia

Two species of albizzia are of great use in the garden, being quick-growing trees with light, feathery attractive foliage. They begin to bloom even as young plants. Though they prefer neutral or rather acidic conditions, they will tolerate mild alkalinity and are more likely to prosper if you add organic materials, such as grape pressings or seaweed, either mixed with the planting earth or as a mulch. Both are good trees for coastal areas.

## Albizia distachya syn. A. lophantha

H 4m/13ft  s 5m/16ft  −3°C/27°F  d f c 2

The plume albizzia is fast-growing, but also very fast-ageing, and will show its suffering in a cold winter. It is useful when young, especially as a quick-growing shelter from sea winds, though it has a tendency to blow over if it grows too richly, and rather quickly becomes unkempt with age. The flowers are fuzzy cylindrical spikes of yellow green.

## Albizia julibrissin

H 10m/33ft  s 12m/40ft  −7°C/19°F  d f c 3

Some varieties of the silk tree form a parasol shape, especially when young. Once established, which is not always easy, it grows fast; you may need to cut back the branches in winter to maintain a graceful shape. The best form is 'Rosea' with rich pink feathery flowers crowded together on top of the branch ends.

## Araucaria heterophylla

H 30m/98ft  s 15m/50ft  −4°C/25°F  d f c

Commonly known as the Norfolk Island pine, this evergreen is widely grown in pots, and makes an interesting plant for indoor or terrace decoration. The container restricts the roots and keeps it to a reasonable height. Planted as an outdoor specimen it will grow, in time, into a very large tree whose symmetrical tiered branches look almost as if they have been deliberately clipped into shape. It grows well in ocean winds, but if not given water and food it tends to sprout back from near the trunk, losing its sculptured look.

## Arbutus unedo

H 6m/20ft  s 6m/20ft  −9°C/16°F  d s c 4

The strawberry tree is a beautiful small evergreen with panicles of small white or pinkish flowers borne in late autumn, at the same time as the previous year's crop of ornamental warty red berries. Although these are edible, they are too dry and pippy to bear very much resemblance to regular strawberries. With age, the bushy look of youth gives way to a gnarled appearance that is most attractive. The tree transplants badly, so if you

*Ailanthus altissima*

want to grow one, obtain a container-grown seedling.

*Arbutus andrachne* is a somewhat taller and broader shrubby tree and there is a beautiful red-trunked cross between the two called *A.* × *andrachnoides*.

## Betula

Birch is a genus which, for the most part, needs cool wet growing conditions. However, *B. albosinensis* (and its subspecies *B. albosinensis septentrionalis*), together with *B. pendula*, will do reasonably well in warmer regions if planted in the cooler, damper corners of the garden.

## Brachychiton

These strange plants, often called 'bottle trees', have grossly swollen trunks. Though usually classed as desert plants, they grow best in hot moist conditions such as they enjoy in their native northeast Queensland. There they drop their leaves and flower in midsummer, and they may also shed their leaves from cold in the winter months.

Brachychitons readily adapt to drought, principally because they have a large taproot which grows well down to reach the moisture in the depths of the soil. They will do well in a hot sunny position but need to be planted in deep soil, not in ground that overlies rock. They should be watered well up to early summer and then not again until the ground begins to dry out the following spring.

Two species are available and are often seen growing in public parks.

### Brachychiton acerifolius

H 15m/50ft  s 10m/33ft  −3°C/27°F  d f 3

The flame tree has large maplelike leaves, and red flowers which completely cover it in some years. Like the smaller *Brachychiton populneus*, which usually has poplar-shaped leaves and greeny-white flowers, it is quick growing, fairly long-lived and can be transplanted in early summer or grown from seed. Beware the hairs in the pods: they can stick into the skin and cause irritation. The brachychitons belong, incidentally, to the same family as the plants that produce the extracts for flavouring Coca-Cola and chocolate.

### Callistemon viminalis

H 7m/23ft  s 5m/16ft  −5°C/23°F  n f c 3

This is a pretty, weeping, small evergreen tree that bears deep purplish-red bottlebrushes through most of the summer months. It grows best with plenty of water and detests wind and drought. It should be pruned when young otherwise it is possible that it will overgrow itself and fall.

### Catalpa bignonioides

H 10m/33ft  s 15m/50ft  −9°C/16°F  o a 2

The Indian bean tree is attractive, deciduous and useful as a shade tree planted around the house. In spring, the wide-spreading branches are densely covered in large heart-shaped leaves above which stand upright panicles of mainly white flowers similar to, but less compact than, the flower spike of the chestnut. It is neither drought nor wind resistant and needs deep soil with occasional watering during summer. As it grows, prune the lower branches until it has formed a trunk 3m/10ft high with a dense canopy under which you can sit and enjoy the cool shade.

### Cedrus libani atlantica

H 30m/98ft  s 30m/98ft  −9°C/16°F  d s

Both this, the Atlas cedar, and the Himalayan *C. deodara* are essentially high-altitude trees that prefer cool moist growing conditions. In dry climates they are slower growing, and the needles are very much shorter than in their native habitat. Even so, the cedars are among the more popular genera for planting in public places. Wherever you see a thriving specimen of the Atlas cedar (or its close relation *C. libani*, the cedar of Lebanon) it is certain to have been planted in a good depth of heavy earth with a moist subsoil.

Numerous different clones have been developed from *C. libani atlantica* and most nurseries now offer a choice both of foliage colour, from dark green to silver, and of shapes – from wide to columnar and from weeping to upright.

### Celtis australis

H 25m/82ft  s 20m/66ft  −8°C/17°F  d a

A magnificent drought-resistant deciduous tree, the Mediterranean hackberry is allied to the elm but has a smooth trunk and in appearance is closer to an old grey beech. It should not be pruned any more than is absolutely necessary but should be allowed to develop its own natural form consisting of a fairly short bole with several massive branches springing from the top. Grown like this it does not split and is robust enough to withstand strong winds. The flowers are so small that you can hardly see them, but the brownish-black fruits, smaller than a cherry stone and sweet, are sometimes eaten by children. The tree seeds itself too freely and is too big for most gardens.

### Ceratonia siliqua

H 8m/26ft  s 10m/33ft  −5°C/23°F  d s

Variously called the carob, the locust bean or St John's bread, this economically valuable tree is widely grown. If it were less common, its beauty would be better appreciated. A dark, dome-shaped evergreen with a twisting (and often hollow) russet trunk, the tree carries green pods which turn brown in autumn all along the branches. These pods now have a variety of uses in the food and plastics industries but in the past they provided a valuable food for cattle and sheep as well as for humans in times of famine. They are sweet and nutritious, but chew one and you will conclude that, when St John fed from this tree in the desert, he must have appreciated his wild honey more than his 'locusts'. In antiquity, the seeds were also used as weights and it is thought that the system of weighing gems and gold in 'carats' derives from the carob.

Quite apart from its fascinating history, the carob makes a good hedge if cut back regularly. Often you will find a dark brown earthy powder of decomposed wood inside the trunk of a mature tree. This is supposed by some to have almost magical qualities as a plant mulch and fertilizer, and can be mixed in with the rest of the

*Ceratonia siliqua*

*Olea europaea* (left) and *Cercis siliquastrum* (right)

soil in your garden. Plants often seem to suffer from a dark mould that faintly blots the foliage and debilitates the tree.

## Cercis siliquastrum
H 7m/23ft S 7m/23ft −9°C/16°F d a 2

Tradition has it that Judas hanged himself from this tree. The story may be doubted since the branches are not very robust. Even so, it is a spectacular small tree and one whose appearance was bound to provoke legend. In spring, usually before the leaves appear, the branches cover themselves with clusters of purple pea-flowers which can be eaten in salads or fritters.

Named clones, or even strains selected for colour, are not easily obtainable. Instead, the trees are grown from seed and the results are not always satisfactory since the colour of the flowers can vary considerably. It is impossible to tell whether a seedling will produce rich purple blooms or pale insignificant ones, unless you choose one that is already in flower. The potted plants should be transplanted in spring and sometimes take a year or two to get established. Though the Judas tree is quite able to look after itself under all reasonable con-ditions, better results will be achieved with a little watering and some shade.

## Citrus
The citrus family includes some of the most marvellous small evergreen trees to be found anywhere in the world. They are beautiful at all times of year, but especially in winter and spring when they are covered in delicious fruits or fragrant white blossoms. Their only drawback is that they are susceptible to cold and disease. The specially selected orange and lemon varieties grown for fruit are all grafted to improve their disease resistance. As an additional disease-control measure, most countries have laws forbidding the importation of citrus plants. Consult a local nursery about the varieties most suited to your conditions.

All citrus trees like moist soil but extremely good drainage. Standing water will kill them, especially if it is in contact with the trunk. The roots extend beyond the outermost tips of the branches, so for watering you should scrape up two circular earth ridges, the first 300mm/12in from the trunk and the other 1m/3ft or so beyond the reach of the branches. Fill this basin every ten days from early spring to midsummer, reducing the frequency to once every three weeks in the absence of rain for the remainder of the year. The water should not stand for more than a few minutes so never provide more than the soil will absorb quickly. The tree is partly dependent on surface roots so avoid cultivating too deeply within an area equal to twice the extent of the branches.

Plant in early spring and ensure that the young tree does not dry out at any moment during the first two summers. Established trees should be given a general fertilizer high in nitrogen, at intervals from late winter to early autumn. Take care only to apply a little at a time since a high concentration of salts in the soil will be injurious. For the same reason, citrus trees are never happy growing in coastal situations. Alkaline conditions call for the application of iron chelate. Big trees can be moved in midsummer. If you do move them, pay great attention to watering.

### Citrus aurantiifolia
H 4m/13ft  S 4m/13ft  −1°C/30°F  o a 1
The lime is the most tender of the citrus fruits, and cannot be recommended for outdoor cultivation in Europe except to enthusiasts who relish a challenge. However, the variety grown in California, 'Bearss Seedless' is said to be as hardy as the lemon.

### Citrus aurantium
H 6m/20ft  S 5m/16ft  −6°C/21°F  o f 1
The Seville or bitter orange is a recognized variety, not just a seedling grown from any orange pip (which normally also produces bitter fruit). The orange-red fruit makes excellent marmalade and liqueurs such as Curaçao. The Seville can also be grown as a fine ornamental tree, or can be clipped to form a hedge or tall screen if plants are spaced at intervals of two-thirds of the height you want them to achieve.

### Citrus limon
H 5m/16ft  S 4m/13ft  −3°C/27°F  o a 1
The lemons are much less hardy than the oranges and will take very little frost, though they mind wind less. They fruit and flower most of the year round.

### × Citrofortunella microcarpa (× C. mitis)
H 4m/13ft  S 3m/10ft  −7°C/19°F  o a 1
The calamondin is said to be the hardiest citrus and is certainly one of the most attractive. The orange or pale pink fruits can be made into marmalade and the flowers are very fragrant. It is a good citrus for pot cultivation and is the one most frequently sold in Europe as an ornamental shrub.

### Citrus × paradisi
H 6m/20ft  S 7m/23ft  −3°C/27°F  o a 2
The large yellow fruit of the grapefruit ripens just before midsummer but only trees growing in regions favoured by long hot summers will bear good crops.

### Citrus reticulata
H 4m/13ft  S 5m/16ft  −5°C/23°F  o a 2
The mandarin is early maturing and the small, sweet, easily peeled fruits are often ready for picking in early winter. It makes a small round tree, rather densely clad in small dark leaves, that flowers in late spring.

### Citrus sinensis
H 4m/13ft  S 4m/13ft  −5°C/23°F  o a 1
This is the tree that produces the sweet orange and, because of its economic importance, dozens of different varieties have been bred, each with its own particular requirements. Specialist producers in orange-growing parts of the world will advise on clones that mature at different dates, and are best suited to the local soils and climate. The two most commonly grown varieties are the Washington Navel and the Valencia, ripening in midwinter and late spring respectively.

### Cupressus
Some people are lovers of conifers, others find them distinctly antipathetic. Certainly, many conifers do not look appropriate alongside dry-climate trees, and collections of multicoloured dwarf conifers usually look out of place even in temperate zones where the climate suits most of them better.

Conifers should be used with care. It is not worth planting any of the many varieties of *Chamaecyparis lawsoniana*, the so-called 'false' cypresses, since they cannot tolerate intense heat. On the other hand, the Italian cypress, or *Cupressus sempervirens*, is a distinctive tree, indigenous to the Mediterranean and adapted to the climate, as is *C. macrocarpa*, the Monterey cypress, in California.

All the cypresses mentioned below make good hedges as well as specimen trees. When pruning, do not cut back beyond the base of the current year's growth. Light clipping can be carried out in autumn, but any heavy pruning should be done in midsummer.

Clippers and shears should be kept sharp and frequently dipped in a strong bleach solution to avoid propagating the fungus disease, *Coryneum* canker *(Seridium cardinale)*, to which they are all – but especially *C. macrocarpa* and *C. sempervirens* – susceptible.

### Cupressus arizonica
H 10m/33ft  S 5m/16ft  −9°C/16°F  d f c
One variety of this tree, usually sold as 'Conica glauca', is much planted in Mediterranean areas because its olivelike silver-grey colour looks rather less out of place than that of some of its conifer cousins. However it

*Citrus limon* in flower

Lemon fruit

*Citrus aurantium*

*Citrus sinensis*

deteriorates with age and tends to become thin and sparse after twenty or thirty years. In its youth, though, it makes an eye-catching pewter-coloured hedge against which the strong reds of hibiscus show up well. It is probably the hardiest of the commonly grown cypresses, and it is claimed that if the wood is well ripened and the tree is growing slowly on dry poor soil it will survive temperatures as low as $-20°C/-3°F$.

### Cupressus macrocarpa

H 20m/66ft  S 20m/66ft  $-9°C/16°F$  d f c

The Monterey cypress is an ugly tree. It is ungainly when young, with stiff branches jutting out too far from the trunk; it is massive but ragged and torn-about when mature. And yet it is useful, making an excellent quickly growing shelter belt in all soils, especially on the coast where it cannot be bettered in this role. In dry unfertilized ground it makes a good hedge, though it easily gets out of control if not cut frequently.

The foliage when crushed has a pungent smell that some people find agreeable. Unfortunately it is susceptible to the fungus disease, *Coryneum* canker, *(Seridium cardinale),* for which there is no cure. Patches of the tree die off and the reddish coloured dead foliage slowly drops. It is best to destroy any infected tree as soon as possible to prevent the disease spreading.

### Cupressus sempervirens

H 20m/66ft  S 5m/16ft  $-9°C/16°F$  d f c

The Italian cypress is probably the best known and most typical tree of the Mediterranean. It is also one of the most useful, making a vertical accent equalled only by the palm. There is enormous variation in the habit and texture of this tree and it is one of the curiosities of gardening that only in Italy has much effort been made to select clones for different shapes or functions, and then only to a limited extent. It is said that the very columnar trees are male and the fatter ones female, but this is based entirely on symbolic association as the tree is bisexual.

Trees grown from seed will be very variable in shape: only some of them will be truly columnar, though they always look narrower when young than when half grown. The proportion of very narrow progeny depends on the quality of the seed and is quite high in the case of some Italian strains. To be certain of acquiring a narrow tree you must buy one that has been grafted; even so, the root stock will have some modifying effect on its form. Best of all are trees grown from cuttings. Although some people believe that plants propagated by this method may blow down more easily, this has not been my experience. In any case, the only way that you can be certain of getting a pair of identical

*Eriobotrya japonica*

trees, to flank a flight of steps or an avenue, for example, is to buy those grown from cuttings from the same parent tree.

Growing conditions also have a profound influence on form. Drought will make for a narrower shape with shorter branches – both of which are desirable characteristics for this cypress.

When buying a tree, go for one that has short dense branches and a strong main leader. Avoid those that have a number of long shoots growing parallel to the main trunk, for when these shoots are larger they will form multiple tops and long side branches that will open in the wind and spoil the look of the tree. Remember that bluish and golden varieties are slower growing.

The Italian cypress is not easy to transplant, especially once it has reached a certain size. Always buy well-established, container-grown trees, not recently dug-up seedlings pushed into a pot for sale. The trees should be planted, if possible, in early autumn – but any time up to the beginning of winter or during late winter and early spring is suitable. Guy or stake the trees very well, keep them well watered, but not waterlogged, and spray the foliage with water as frequently as you can.

Once established the trees should be watered very occasionally and given little or no fertilizer. For a quick screen you can plant specimens 250mm/10in away from each other. Plant 1m/3ft apart for a dense high wall and at twice that distance for a windbreak. For a really dense screen, choose plants that have foliage down to the ground, although it is attractive in certain situations to cut off all the lower branches up to, say, 2.5m/8ft from the ground. Neither this, nor any other cypress, will stand shade, and an Italian cypress planted against a house will lose all foliage from that side.

The pollen from the male flowers is produced in such quantities in early spring that the trees sometimes look as if they are burning when the laden catkins are shaken in a sudden breeze. Cones are usually produced in abundance and can grow as large as a golf ball; at this size they are rather ornamental. They open in the second year and may remain on the tree almost indefinitely. Since they tend to weigh down the branches and open out the very columnar trees, varieties have been selected that bear few or no cones.

### Diospyros kaki

H 10m/33ft  S 10m/33ft  −5°C/23°F  n a 4

The persimmon is an easily grown deciduous tree of moderate size that benefits from rich soil and more than the occasional watering. It is handsome at all times of the year but especially in late autumn when the leaf changes colour and the fruit is displayed. The fruit is about the size of a tomato but a prettier red-orange. Some find its taste and texture addictive, others find it blandly jellified. Most people find it good when dried; the fruit should be cut with the stalk attached when red but still hard, peeled and hung in the sun. Male trees do not bear fruit so you need to buy a named female variety; usually these are grafted on the stock of *D. virginiana*, which has smaller fruit and less intense autumn colour. This particular species has other disadvantages: the flower, fruit and leaf drop is messy; the flowers are toxic to bees, and both the flowers and the leaves will kill fish if they fall into a pond in any quantity.

### Elaeagnus angustifolia

H 6m/20ft  S 6m/20ft  −9°C/16°F  d f c 2

The oleaster or Russian olive is a silver-leaved deciduous bush or small tree, resistant to most difficult conditions, including cold and coastal wind or salt. It will stand clipping into a medium height hedge or barrier. The very fragrant small flowers are borne in late spring, followed by olivelike fruit. It will not live long in regions that have no winter frosts.

### Eriobotrya japonica

H 6m/20ft  S 6m/20ft  −7°C/19°F  o a c 4

The loquat is a small pretty evergreen with large ribbed

*Erythrina crista-galli*

and toothed leaves. These are light greenish-grey when young, turning dark green and rusty beneath later on. Clumps of white, furry fragrant flowers emerge in early winter and swell to tasty orange fruit with large brown seeds in early summer. These may be of an acceptable size and taste on seedlings but are much bigger and better on named loquat varieties. Once established the tree is drought resistant but will do better if watered regularly. It should be sprayed twice a year with fungicide to avoid the blackening of the leaves and fruit.

### Erythrina crista-galli

H 4m/13ft  S 4m/13ft  −2°C/28°F  o a c 3

This small to medium-sized shrub will form a small tree in frost-free regions. The spectacular scarlet 'flamingo-beak' flowers cluster at the branch ends. In places that are not quite frost-free you can treat it as a perennial, cutting it back to a stump in winter. Cutting the branches back after flowering often induces a second flush.

### Eucalyptus

There are about 450 eucalypt species, varying from some of the largest trees on earth to low stragglers that reach a mere 2m/6ft.

Many people feel that the distinctive look of eucalypts does not fit well with trees such as the olive, holm

*Eucalyptus ficifolia*

oak and Aleppo pine. Though this may be true of many eucalypts, nonetheless there are some that may be grown to advantage, providing a service that few other trees can. The two most frequently planted are *E. camaldulensis* (syn. *E. rostrata*), a tough tree with greedy roots that grows tall and well under varying conditions, and *E. globulus*. However, the latter is far from ideal as it is susceptible to chlorosis, has greedy roots, messy falling leaves and stripping bark. Better than either is *E. gomphocephala*. Not only is it particularly good in limestone and near the sea, it also flowers when very young. All three are much too big for most gardens, where you should plant one of the following smaller species.

**Eucalyptus caesia**
H 5m/16ft  s 4m/13ft  −5°C/23°F  d f 1
This forms a large grey-green bush, weeping and graceful, with pink-rose flowers during winter.

**Eucalyptus ficifolia**
H 8m/26ft  s 8m/26ft  −3°C/27°F  a 2
This eucalyptus is variable from seed, so if you want to be sure of a good red flower (the most sought-after colour) purchase a specimen already in bloom. It does not do well in alkaline soil.

**Eucalyptus torquata**
H 6m/20ft  s 4m/13ft  −3°C/27°F  d f c
This bears small coral-red blossoms for most of the year and contributes a light and graceful effect to the garden. The foliage of the head needs occasional pruning or the tree may blow over.

**Ficus carica**
H 7m/23ft  s 9m/30ft  −8°C/17°F  d f c
The edible fig is a curious tree. Though the wood is pithy it lives to a great age and becomes attractively gnarled in old specimens. It is one of the few deciduous members of a predominantly evergreen genus. Garden varieties are all female and self-fertilizing but the Smyrna varieties, used to produce dried figs, rely on fig wasps which live only on male trees to fertilize them.

The fruit, enjoyed since antiquity, is delicious, and comes in two crops: the first in midsummer on last year's wood, the second in early autumn from the current year's growth. Winter temperatures of much below − 4°C/25°F will kill the branches and, in these conditions, the plant will become a shrub of annual growth and will not bear fruit. For best fruiting the tree needs very little fertilizer, well-drained soil, occasional watering up to late summer and light pruning just to form and open the tree.

It should also be noted that the fallen fruits are messy, the hairy leaves may irritate the skin, the milky sap is somewhat poisonous and the roots are greedy and invasive. But the broad overlapping leaves provide welcome summer shade.

## Ficus elastica

H 8m/26ft S 6m/20ft −2°C/28°F o a

The rubber plant, so popular indoors, will grow as a small tree outdoors in frost-free gardens, normally in the unselected form, which has longer, lighter-coloured leaves than indoor varieties such as 'Decora'. It has invasive roots and is liable to be cut hard back even by light frosts.

## Ficus retusa nitida

H 8m/26ft S 8m/26ft −3°C/27°F o f

This dark evergreen tree (syn. *F. microcarpa nitida*) has shining leaves finely drawn out at the tip and the base. It is an attractive clean tree that will take shearing and prosper in containers. It is much planted as a street tree in California and often cut into topiary shapes.

## Fraxinus uhdei

H 18m/60ft S 15m/50ft −6°C/21°F d f c

The Mexican ash tree is fast growing, capable of reaching 10m/33ft in ten years. It grows easily from seed, is drought resistant and normally free of diseases or pests, though it has greedy roots. It makes a useful screen and looks deciduous but is more or less evergreen, only losing its bright green leaves after a frost or just before the new foliage appears in early spring. The growth is upright in young trees, beginning to spread with age.

## Ginkgo biloba

H 18m/60ft S 15m/50ft −9°C/16°F d a 4

The maidenhair tree is the only species of its order, now that botanists have established that it is not a member of the yew family. It has an ancient pedigree and fossil relatives have been traced back to the Jurassic. The light green fan-shaped leaves turn golden in autumn, making it a distinctive ornamental garden tree. It is best to plant only a graft or cutting from a known male tree. The fruits of the female tree smell unpleasant though the edible kernel is esteemed in Japan. The ginkgo needs watering well until established. Its shape varies; 'Fastigiata' is a good columnar form.

## Gleditsia triacanthos

H 20m/66ft S 15m/50ft −9°C/16°F d f c

This large North American tree has feathery foliage and casts a light shade under which grass will happily grow. Consequently the honey locust is a good specimen tree for the lawn; it is easy to grow and will accept most conditions. There are two thornless varieties: 'Inermis' and 'Sunburst'. When young, the latter has bright yellow leaves that turn to light green in summer. Occasional watering results in even faster development

*Ficus elastica*

but the greedy roots demand room and will lift paving if planted too close.

## Hakea laurina

H 7m/23ft S 7m/23ft −4°C/25°F d a c 1

Hakeas have acacialike foliage but produce unusual pincushion flowers all along the branches in winter; in *H. laurina*, the sea urchin tree, the cushion is crimson with yellow pins. Though said to do badly in alkaline soil, *H. laurina* and the white-flowered *H. saligna* both grow well if given an occasional dose of iron chelate. *H. laurina* is easy to grow from seed, resistant to drought, and tolerant of poor soil and salt winds, though it is liable to blow over if not pruned in early years.

## Jacaranda mimosifolia

H 12m/40ft S 10m/33ft −3°C/27°F o f c 3

For many people there is no more beautiful flowering tree than the jacaranda. The ferny foliage gives a pleasant light shade, and the pale purple-blue flowers that cover the tree in early summer are of an exquisite hue. It has only one fault: spent flowers, leaflets and leafstalks can make a mess at times. The blue carpet of fallen flowers is not unattractive, but the leaves continue falling all through the winter until the tree is left bare in early spring. The jacaranda will resist a few degrees of frost, though the tips of the branches may die, and the

*Koelreuteria bipinnata*

tree is more tender when young. Be sparing with fertilizer and do not water after midsummer.

### Juniperus

This genus is more fully treated with the Shrubs (pages 95-96) but one or two make useful small trees. *Juniperus chinensis* can reach 20m/66ft in the wild but two of the varieties selected from it – 'Keteleeri' and 'Kaizuka' – are smaller and more suitable for gardens, 'Keteleeri' makes a blue-green cone and produces tiny blue-green fruits, while 'Kaizuka' has a twisted form, highly esteemed in California. *J. scopulorum* 'Blue Heaven' and *J. scopulorum* 'Skyrocket' are narrow silvery blue pyramidal trees that reach 6m/20ft. All are drought resistant and like a well-drained, alkaline soil.

### Koelreuteria bipinnata

H 10m/33ft  S 12m/40ft  −7°C/19°F  o f c 3
The golden rain tree is said to require a lime-free soil, but it does well on alkaline soils on Mallorca and very quickly forms a pretty medium-sized deciduous tree as wide as it is high. Large panicles of small golden flowers, in late summer, are followed by dull-red seed pods shaped like Chinese lanterns. The pods seem to differ in the intensity of their colouring between one tree and another but the better examples are very showy. *K. paniculata* is perhaps better known but has

less spectacular brown pods. Both grow fast from seed and flower when young, sometimes within three years of germination. They show autumn colour briefly, and make ideal patio or lawn trees. Both are better for occasional watering, especially when young.

### Lagerstroemia indica

H 7m/23ft  S 6m/20ft  −3°C/27°F  m s 3
The crape myrtle is a very beautiful small tree or large deciduous shrub, with large heads of small crinkled flowers that last through the late summer and into autumn. Flower colours range from white, through pink and rose, to red and violet, all with a distinctive luminous quality. The myrtle looks exquisite trained to grow as a tree, with its smooth bark, blotched with brown, grey and pink. New growths in spring are bronze coloured and in autumn the leaf tones range through yellow and red. Although moderately drought resistant it is much happier for fairly frequent deep watering. Any sign of chlorosis is easily corrected with iron chelate.

### Lagunaria patersonii

H 12m/40ft  S 9m/30ft  −3°C/27°F  d f c 2
This medium-sized evergreen tree is sometimes called the Norfolk Island hibiscus and is known in California as the primrose tree. Both names rather overstate its

floral abilities which are good but not outstanding. The other Californian name, the 'cow-itch tree', seems more in keeping for the seed pod is full of irritating hairs. It has grey-green leaves and is fast growing, narrow in youth and spreading with age. The flowers are pinkish, fading white, and about 50mm/2in in diameter. It is very good on the coast, resisting wind and salt, and it also copes well with heat and drought.

## Laurus nobilis
H 12m/40ft  S 10m/33ft  −7°C/19°F  d s c 1
The bay tree has been grown since antiquity and is a member of the rather select club of non-coniferous evergreen trees. It is accommodating and will adapt to most soils and conditions; it needs no watering in the summer and has considerable resistance to shade and coastal salt spray. This adaptability extends to a useful range of shapes: it can be trained as a small sphere, only 750mm/30in high or as an attractive small tree, and will make a good hedge of almost any size.

It is one of the best shrubs for breaking up a long wall. If it is planted in the angle of a wall, the foliage facing the masonry will not die for lack of light, unlike that of the Italian cypress. As well as providing an essential ingredient of the cook's *bouquet garni*, the bay tree flowers in late winter. The clusters of yellow blossoms along the branches are quite showy, as are the black berries that follow them.

A native of the Mediterranean, the bay was much appreciated by the ancient Greeks and Romans, being the 'laurel' used to crown heroes and poets. It was also believed that the tree was never struck by lightning and the Roman emperor Tiberius wore a bay wreath as an insurance against such a calamity.

## Magnolia grandiflora
H 30m/98ft  S 20m/66ft  −9°C/16°F  o s c 3
A native of the southeastern United States, *M. grandiflora* is a magnificent evergreen tree with huge thick glossy green leaves, usually reddy-brown beneath. When its enormous fragrant white flowers bloom in summer, it is very beautiful. The flowers are followed by woody fruit capsules, rather like pine cones in appearance, that split all over to show the scarlet seeds. Although a tree of great distinction, it is hard to make it prosper. It likes moist air, and is happy on the coast. It needs a good depth of moist, well-drained soil, and benefits from organic mulches spread around the roots. An occasional application of iron chelate will help to keep it dense and healthy. Its roots are shallow, so do not go too close with motor cultivators.

## Melia azedarach
H 10m/33ft  S 10m/33ft  −9°C/16°F  d f 2
Commonly known as the Chinaberry or bead tree, this is a tough fast-growing deciduous tree that is resistant to drought and needs little care. It is widely used as a street tree in southern Europe and makes an attractive shade tree for the larger garden. Its fragrant lilac flowers appear in spring at the same time as the dark green bipinnate leaves begin to open; in winter the bare branches are hung with open bunches of yellow berries, with fluted seeds once used to make rosary beads.

*M. azedarach* is well worth planting in difficult

*Laurus nobilis*

*Magnolia grandiflora*

*Melia azedarach*

and some moisture, it will accept drought and heavier soils. It does quite well, and will flower, in a pot, and in areas susceptible to frost it is often grown as a shrub for the conservatory.

## Olea europaea

The olive exists in three very different forms, all evergreen and hardy to −8°C/17°F: the cultivated gnarled tree, sometimes very ancient, that produces the olives that are eaten or pressed for oil; the wild olive with narrower pointed leaves and much smaller worthless fruit; and the odd little tree that is hardly recognizable as an olive at all, dense and often only a few centimetres high.

Old olives seem to look best in a dry glade, spaced regularly about 10m/33ft apart. An isolated specimen on a rich green watered lawn (where it will not thrive), or mixed up with flowering shrubs and perennials, looks rather incongruous. Olives can be moved easily, and, provided that the tree is properly prepared, can be planted at most times of year, though early spring is generally best.

## Parkinsonia aculeata

H 7m/23ft  S 10m/33ft  −4°C/25°F  d f c 3

In a sunny spot in a warm climate this makes a pretty and resilient small evergreen tree. The general effect is charmingly diaphanous. Tiny leaves on long midribs throw a light shade and delicate yellow flowers touched with orange bloom from spring to autumn. It needs no watering and grows well on alkaline soils.

## Paulownia tomentosa

H 15m/50ft  S 15m/50ft  −7°C/19°F  o f 2

This large deciduous shade tree has spectacular violet foxglovelike flowers that form as fat buds in autumn and open in spring as the leaves unfold. The elongated heart-shaped leaves can be very large and dense on a healthy, vigorous tree. However, *P. tomentosa* may be hard to grow: it needs deep, fertile soil that is not too calcareous, and some dampness at the roots, especially when young. Enormous leaves will grow on the thick annual shoots if the young tree is cut right back. This can then be done every year or two, though the striking foliage effect is obtained at the expense of flowers.

## Persea americana

H 10m/33ft  S 12m/40ft  −4°C/25°F  m f c

The avocado pear is now widely cultivated commercially, and many people have grown trees from seeds. Although these make good looking shade trees, only grafted plants produce good-quality fruit. The main

sites. It does not mind alkaline soils and has few disadvantages, other than a tendency to sucker, and to seed itself. The seeding is helped by birds who like the fruit – though for animals and humans it is poisonous. The branches are brittle and may break in wind.

## Metrosideros excelsus

H 20m/66ft  S 24m/80ft  −2°C/28°F  o s c 2

The common name for this beautiful evergreen is the 'New Zealand Christmas Tree' – reminding us that Christmas in New Zealand occurs in midsummer, which is when the spectacular clusters of tight, fuzzy, rather eucalyptuslike dark red flowers appear. If left to grow naturally, *M. excelsus* forms a twisting woody bush. However, given time, it can be trained to a tree that may reach 20m/66ft. It has hanging aerial roots and extremely hard wood.

*M. excelsus* will grow fairly easily, if slowly, from seed. The juvenile growth is dark green and brilliantly shiny. After about two years this gives way to grey-green adult foliage that is extremely resistant to salt winds and even to salt spray. Although it prefers sandy loams

*Pinus halepensis*

requirement of this evergreen is perfect drainage: it needs watering frequently, but the soil must not be allowed to get too wet. It is not fond of alkaline soils but will grow in them if dosed from time to time with iron chelate. Rich organic feeding is much appreciated. The tree itself will not be hurt by the cold in any region where orange trees grow, but more than a light frost will kill the flowers. There are many varieties ('Hass' is one of the best) and there are different root stocks for different conditions. If you want fruit consult your nursery about the best choice for your area, otherwise simply plant a seed for fun and shade.

## Pinus

Pine trees in general like sun and good drainage but, with some outstanding exceptions described below, they are unhappy in extremes of heat or drought. Most grow best with occasional deep watering. They are not easy to transplant except from pots or shallow restricted soils, and even then it is safer to move them in early autumn. Low-nitrogen fertilizer can be applied in the poorest of soils, otherwise they are better without.

All pines in the Mediterranean suffer from the ravages of *Thaumetopoea pityocampa*, the processionary caterpillar, against which there is at the moment no easy remedy. When the caterpillars hatch in the summer they form unsightly cobwebby nests in the tree, which they then go on to strip of needles. Later they march about in a single file of great length. It is not, unfortunately, the case that if you join the head to the tail of the file, they will march round in circles until dead of exhaustion! Do not touch them, for they are covered in irritating hairs, and the only bird that will eat them is the hoopoe. If possible, prune out and destroy the nests.

### Pinus canariensis
H 25m/82ft  S 15m/50ft  −8°C/17°F  d f c
The Canary Island pine is an erect, shaggy but elegant tree with long, rather greyish needles, that will grow in most warm climates. It is a useful tree that, with a little watering, will grow quickly in the early years. It will take very hard pruning.

### Pinus halepensis
H 20m/66ft  S 15m/50ft  −7°C/19°F  d f c
The Aleppo pine will grow in any kind of soil. It needs

little water or food and can withstand extreme exposure to wind or salt. For that reason, old gnarled specimens are often seen growing in landscapes where no other trees will thrive. If you want a tall tree, cut off the lower branches in late winter to encourage upward growth.

**Pinus pinea**
H 25m/82ft S 25m/82ft −9°C/16°F o f c
The umbrella pine is so called because of its characteristic domed shape. Cut off the lower branches in late winter if you want it to assume this shape and make a dense, shady crown. Early growth is rapid and there is no advantage to be gained by paying more for a big plant, since a small one will probably have grown just as well after a few years. In fact this tree will eventually become too big for all but the largest gardens. However, young specimens are just as attractive as mature adults. The umbrella pine likes deep sandy soil and some moisture at the roots. Also known as the Italian stone pine, this is the tree that yields the edible seeds sold as pine kernels.

**Pittosporum tenuifolium**
H 5m/16ft S 2.5m/8ft −7°C/19°F n a c
Not only an excellent seaside hedge or small shade tree, its small wavy edged leaves on black branchlets are also ideal for flower arrangements. Nursery gardens often stock one of its many grey-green variegated forms.

**Pittosporum tobira**
H 8m/26ft S 8m/26ft −7°C/19°F o f c 2
When young, this is an invaluable shrub, with lustrous dark green leaves. In time it becomes a small tree with small grey-green leaves and much character. At both stages it bears small scented white flowers in dense clusters in spring. It is indifferent to salt wind and to most diseases, except aphids and scale, and, although much happier when given occasional watering, it will take a period of drought. If you want to contain the growth, prune out unwanted branches, but do not shear indiscriminately.

*P. undulatum* is a similar species that forms fragrant white flowers followed by clusters of orange berries.

**Platanus × acerifolia**
H 30m/98ft S 25m/82ft −9°C/16°F d f 4
The plane tree was much favoured by the ancient Greeks, and it is easy to understand why. This tree is resistant to drought, impartial as to soil, is fast growing and long-lived, can be cut about as much as you will, and transplants at any size. It is also able to withstand air pollution.

This plane is attractive at all seasons. In spring the

*Prunus serrulata*

pale green leaves unfold against the mottled brown and white trunk; in summer it gives a moderate and extensive shade; in autumn the leaves turn various hues of golden brown; and in winter the branches are hung with groups of long-stalked seed balls. By removing the branches fairly close to the top of the trunk, and then performing a similar pruning operation on the roots, you can transplant a mature tree, even one with a trunk as wide as 1m/3ft in diameter. If kept well watered for a couple of years in its new site, it will soon make a large tree again. Once established the plane tree will resist drought, but it will grow faster and more strongly with occasional watering.

**Populus alba**
H 20m/66ft S 20m/66ft −9°C/16°F d f c
The white poplar takes its name from the colour of the bark and the undersides of its leaves. Its resistance to sea winds makes it an invaluable shelter belt tree. It is good on chalk, and withstands drought, although it will grow much larger with some water. The only disadvantage is that root suckers are produced in quantity,

*Punica granatum*

especially round a cut tree. The columnar form, *P. alba* 'Pyramidalis' (still most often sold under the old name of *P. bolleana*) is useful as an accent tree.

### Prunus cerasifera 'Pissardii'
H 6m/20ft  S 6m/20ft  −9°C/16°F  o a 1
This popular and easily grown flowering cherry provides an attractive display of pink flowers against ruby-red young foliage which later turns through wine-red to dull brown-purple. Japanese cherries derive from *P. serrulata* whose flowers of white to deep pink are unsurpassed in their profusion.

### Prunus dulcis
H 8m/26ft  S 8m/26ft  −9°c/16°f  d a 1
The almond is cultivated throughout the Mediterranean wherever you find deep, well-drained soil, high summer heat and no late winter frosts to damage the developing fruit. It provides the first flowers of spring. They are white or very pale pink in most fruiting varieties, but bright pink in some. Most are self-sterile, so plant two different varieties together.

### Punica granatum
H 5m/16ft  S 4m/13ft  −7°C/19°F  o a
The fruit of the pomegranate is more pip than apple, but the tree is well worth planting for its ornamental value. The red-bronze colour of the new spring foliage and the clear yellows of the dying leaves in autumn are delightful. This tree also has beautiful, though not abundant, brilliant red flowers in early summer. These are followed by the large round colourful fruits. *P. granatum nana* is a dwarf variety that grows to about 1m/3ft: it is supposed to come true from seed, though this supposition is not entirely reliable.

There are also double-flowered ornamental forms in various colours that do not set fruit. The plants can be cut into hedges and, though they are deciduous, they are sufficiently twiggy to give some barrier effect even in winter. Pomegranates tolerate (even need) summer heat and alkaline conditions. Though they will grow without any watering they are better for an occasional deep soak.

### Quercus ilex
H 20m/66ft  S 20m/66ft  −9°C/16°F  d s c
The holm oak is a stately evergreen that was once very common in the wild in Mediterranean regions but the high value of its wood resulted in widespread felling. Though drought resistant in summer, it is only really happy in regions of substantial winter rainfall. The glossy leaves have grey-felted undersides and are very diverse in shape and size so that an opportunity exists to select clones for garden use.

Holm oaks suffer from a fungus that begins to affect trees as they reach maturity and gives them a distinctive bare-branched look. The application of fungicide, either as a spray over the foliage or sprinkled on the roots, appears to effect some improvement. One variety has sweet edible acorns that can be toasted and taste not unlike almonds.

### Robinia pseudoacacia
H 25m/82ft  S 20m/66ft  −9°C/16°F  d f c 2
The false acacia is a very pretty deciduous tree that provides light shade and bears plentiful heads of scented white pea-flowers in the middle of spring. Since it suckers and seeds freely, and as both the suckers and the young trees are spiny and painful to remove, it is probably better left to the wilder margins of your garden. The variety called 'Bessoniana' is slightly smaller and has spineless branches, while 'Frisia' has rich yellow foliage. Other clones have attractive pink or bright purple flowers.

*Sophora japonica*

### Salix × sepulcralis 'Chrysocoma'

H 15m/50ft  S 15m/50ft  −9°C/16°F  o f c

For a plant that is usually associated with water this hybrid deciduous willow and its parents, *S. alba* and *S. babylonica*, do unexpectedly well under dry conditions, though they then make trees of only half the usual dimensions. They need occasional watering and will grow faster and to a larger size if their roots are kept moist. Their light green weeping form provides an interesting foil to the dark spires of Italian cypress. It is advisable to plant them well away from the house, because they have ravenous roots that relentlessly seek out water and frequently cause blocked drains.

The natural form of the tree can be improved by training the main stem against a stout post until it reaches a height of 4m/13ft before you allow it to arch over and weep. *S. babylonica pekinensis* 'Tortuosa' (syn. *S. matsudana* 'Tortuosa') is a narrow small tree, fairly resistant to drought and with curious contorted and twisted branches. These make an attractive winter silhouette and are useful in flower arrangements, especially when the catkins are borne in spring.

### Schinus molle

H 12m/40ft  S 15m/50ft  −6°C/21°F  d a c 4

This is a deservedly popular small evergreen tree, easy to grow, drought resistant, disease free, tough and very attractive in a quiet way with its weeping feathery foliage, loose panicles of small red berries and, in time, a gnarled almost olivelike trunk. The pronounced peppery taste of the seeds accounts for its common name:

'the pepper tree'. Points against it are rather slow growth, the often dull yellow-green colour of the foliage and the need to plant several trees if you want good crops of berries, even though the tree is, in fact, bisexual. The tree is completely resistant to drought thanks to its very powerful far-ranging root system, but this can cause problems with drains and walls. It also casts off a great deal of litter which renders the ground beneath it acidic and unacceptable to many plants. It thrives on heat, and below-zero temperatures will cause it to shed its leaves.

### Sophora japonica

H 15m/50ft  S 15m/50ft  −9°C/16°F  d f 4

This oriental deciduous tree is drought and heat resistant and provides good shade. The pealike flowers are not very showy; more so are the beanlike fruit pods which are yellow with constrictions between the seeds and cover the tree. A number of varieties exist; the most common is *S. japonica* 'Pendula' which, with a little training and support, will make a large parasol or, grown over a pergola, a shady summer bower. Two other species worth trying are *S. secundiflora*, a large healthy evergreen shrub that will, if trained, make a small tree with fragrant purple flowers but poisonous red seeds, and *S. tetraptera*, a half-deciduous small wispy tree that needs shade and dampness but has beautiful hanging golden bell flowers in spring. Both these trees are slow growing, rather tender and need occasional summer irrigation.

### Tamarix

H 4m/13ft  S 3m/10ft  −9°C/16°F  d f c

This genus of shrubs or small trees would win any competition for resistance to sea spray, drought and wind and is therefore invaluable for coastal planting. The taxonomy of the tamarisks is complex but for garden purposes they can be divided into those that flower in spring on last year's wood, and those that flower in summer and early autumn on the current year's wood. Even this is not a completely reliable division, since some species do both. All are approximately the same size and have similar characteristics.

*T. parviflora* and the related *T. tetrandra* belong to the spring-flowering group which needs pruning and forming as soon as the pink flowers are over.

The autumn-flowering group is represented by *T. ramosissima* 'Rosea' (usually sold as *T. pentandra*), a beautiful shrub bearing pink flowers in late summer and best hard-pruned in late winter. Another member of this group is *T. gallica*, but its close relative *T. africana*

*Tamarix pentandra* hovers gracefully over zonal pelargoniums

may conform to either group, depending on when it is pruned.

Although resistant to drought, tamarisks will all grow best with some watering. They are easily propagated by detaching a branch, sticking it in the ground and keeping it watered. You can make a good seaside hedge very quickly in this way. Their natural growth is shrublike and you will have to train your plant to make a tree.

### Thuja orientalis syn. **Platycladus orientalis**

H 12m/40ft  S 4m/13ft  −9°C/16°F  o a

This is one of the best conifers, for it is resistant to heat and drought and its roots do not spread. There is a wealth of varieties to choose from, ranging in size and shape from a yellow football to a small dense tree, similar to the wild Chinese form, that may reach 12m/40ft tall. The low-growing kinds can be used to make a hedge that hardly needs shearing.

### Ulmus parvifolia

H 12m/40ft  S 10m/33ft  −9°C/16°F  o f c

The Chinese elm is a pretty, fast-growing, small-leaved tree of medium size that is evergreen in some examples, such as *U. parvifolia* 'Sempervirens' and *U. parvifolia* 'True Green', but deciduous in others, depending on heredity and the degree of winter cold.

*Phoenix canariensis* towers over *Agave americana* in a Menton garden

# PALMS, SWORD PALMS AND CYCADS

Although often all loosely called palms, these are three different and unrelated groups of plants. The true palms, members of the family *Palmae*, may be divided into two groups: those sometimes called feather palms that have pinnate leaves with a central midrib, and in some of which either side of the leaf is divided into leaflets; and those called fan palms because of their palmate leaves with veins or leaflets radiating from a central point like the fingers of a hand. Cycads are primitive plants most closely related to conifers and often resembling feather palms. The sword palms belong to the agave family and have long, narrow leaves growing in terminal tufts from the ends of the branches.

The transplanting of all of these requires care, but is not difficult. If certain rules are followed, trees of any size can be moved. The main problems are those of transporting the trees and guying them down.

First, they should only be moved in the summer. Their roots die when they are moved, and there must be sufficient warmth for new roots to grow before the cold comes. Second (and in this they are quite distinct from all woody trees), it is of benefit to plant them up to 1m/3ft deeper than they were before they were dug up. Third, you should leave the leaves tied up around the crown, to protect it, for a year after planting. The palm has only one growing point, the crown, and if this dies, so does the tree.

Finally, you must secure the tree so that the lower trunk will not move within the earth, for if it does the fleshy new roots will be rubbed off and the tree will not 'take'. A metal collar fitted around the trunk provides an effective means of anchoring the tree. You should be able to get a blacksmith to make one for you. Ask him to make it only slightly larger than the circumference of the trunk, measured a third of the way down from the head, and in two halves that can be bolted together. It should have welded to it four eyes from which you can lead thick wire cable, or light metal rods, to suitable attachment points on the ground or adjacent walls. Wooden wedges inside the collar, lightly tapped home, will stop it from chafing the trunk; this is, in any case, not so susceptible to damage as is the tender growing layer, the cambium, that lies just inside the trunk of a woody tree.

**Arecastrum romanzoffianum**
(now correctly **Syagrus romanzoffiana**)
H 12m/40ft  S 8m/26ft  −4°C/25°F  o f
The queen palm deserves to be used more, because it grows quickly and has a graceful feathery form that gives a tropical effect and casts a light shade. It is useful for smallish gardens, courtyards or around pools, and looks good in groups (planted 4m/13ft apart). Avoid positions exposed to strong winds. Many nurseries sell this palm under the name *Cocos plumosa*.

**Beaucarnea recurvata**
H 5m/16ft  S 4m/13ft  −5°C/23°F  d s c
This dramatic sword palm, with its huge swollen base and feathery top, looks as though it comes from another planet; however, the bottle ponytail is surprisingly tolerant of earthly climates. If it gets full sun, good drainage and only occasional deep watering in summer, it should be hardy to at least −5°C/23°F. It is an excellent house or container plant if not over-watered, and in time makes an extraordinary inhabitant for the garden.

**Chamaerops humilis**
H 4m/13ft  S 1.5m/5ft  −9°C/16°F  d s c
The European fan palm grows wild in the western Mediterranean region. In dry, rocky places it never becomes more than a dwarf tree but under cultivation it can reach 5m/16ft. It often grows in clumps and these look well in gardens, although each palm takes years to grow; insufficiently controlled transplanting by impatient gardeners has made large wild specimens a rarity. It can be distinguished from the similar *Trachycarpus fortunei* by its spiny leaf stalks.

Other popular fan palms include species of thrinax and coccothrinax, often with silvery blue-green leaves.

*Chamaerops humilis* (in the background) and *Brahea armata* (right foreground)

**Chrysalidocarpus lutescens**
H 6m/20ft S 3m/10ft −2°C/28°F m f
The clump-forming bamboo palm is good as an elegant, quick-developing decoration for a sheltered terrace. The trunks will eventually become 200mm/8in in diameter. The roots must have perpetually damp conditions when growing. For this reason it is not always a success in a pot, but will do well planted in a hole in the paving. Frost will burn some of the leaves but, if only slight, should not affect its growth. It likes a little shade and has long been a favourite for the house, but, sadly, it is seldom used as an outdoor plant.

**Cordyline australis**
H 8m/26ft S 4m/13ft −7°C/19°F d a c
The cabbage palm looks like a frondy version of a yucca, as does *C. indivisa*, with soft leaves up to 1m/3ft long. It makes an excellent specimen plant and is cheap, tough and easily transplanted. *C. australis* branches more than *C. indivisa*. It has narrower leaves (around 50mm/2in), is more often found in nurseries and is,

perhaps, rather more useful in gardens than *C. indivisa*. It grows well in tubs, in rocky, desertlike cactus gardens and can tolerate coastal conditions. *C. australis* usually begins to branch, once it has flowered, at a height of 3m/10ft or so. But branching can be induced earlier in this sword palm by cutting out the growing point when the plant is young, something you cannot do with a palm proper.

**Cycas revoluta**
H 3m/10ft S 2m/6ft −8°C/17°F o s c
The sago palm is a very slow-growing, primitive cycad. Nurseries charge a great deal even for small specimens consisting only of a tuft of tough fernlike leaves arching out from a bulblike base. After many years it will form a trunk and in due course the plant will look like a small palm. It is tough but prefers moist organic lightish soil, moist air and light shade. In its early years the sago palm makes an excellent large pot plant providing a dramatic focal point with its attractive leaves produced in annual whorls.

## Phoenix

The date palm, *Phoenix dactylifera*, looks remarkably similar to the coconut palm and has similar attractive associations – with desert oases and hot sun. As they are fairly easily transplanted even when fully grown, date palms give gardeners in hot, dry climates the means to create immediate tropical effects. *P. canariensis*, the Canary palm, and *P. dactylifera*, the source of edible dates, differ in that the former is much heavier and more robust, with a thicker trunk and a denser head. In fact, though, with an eventual height of 15m/50ft and a spread of 13m/43ft, the Canary palm is too big for all but large gardens. It is majestic rather than graceful.

The leaflets of the Canary palm, growing off the central rib of the leaf, almost meet along their sides and are deep green, whereas the leaflets of the date palm are well-separated and grey-green. The two species hybridize easily and many of the palms you see are intermediate between the two. They stay close to the ground while their head of fronds is growing. When the head has reached full size, after perhaps five or six years, the trunk starts to grow upwards at a rate of around 300mm/12in per year. Modified leaflets at the bases of the larger fronds form sharp spines and wounds caused by these seem to take an abnormally long time to heal.

The miniature date palm, *P. roebelenii*, is altogether more graceful than the preceding sorts although it is not quite so hardy.

*Cycas revoluta, Euphorbia candelabrum erythraea* (right)

Male *Cycas revoluta* in flower

Phoenix species are not the only feather palms widely grown around the Mediterranean: the Yatay palm, *Butia capitata*, with its elegant blue-green foliage on a relatively large tree, is one of the most popular.

### Phoenix dactylifera,
H 20m/66ft S 6m/20ft −5°C/23°F d a c
The edible date palm only fruits properly when the summer is really hot; in any case, you need specially selected, named varieties for successful fruiting, and these are hard to get. Even so, the species is attractive and a good choice if you live near the sea because it is very resistant to salty coastal conditions.

### Trachycarpus fortunei
H 8m/26ft S 3m/10ft −9°C/16°F d s c i
The Chusan palm is the hardiest of all the palms – it will survive temperatures of −17°C/2°F when mature. It will grow to 15m/50ft but is unlikely to exceed 8m/26ft in dry climates. When mature it has a distinctively slender trunk with a spherical mop of fan leaves at the top. The trunk increases in diameter with

*Washingtonia filifera*

*Yucca aloifolia*

*Yucca gloriosa*

height and is covered with black fibrous hair that, in its native China, is made into rope and coarse cloth.

## Washingtonia filifera
H 18m/60ft  S 5m/16ft  −8°C/17°F  o f c
and
## Washingtonia robusta
H 30m/98ft  S 5m/16ft  −5°C/23°F  d f c
These big fan palms come, broadly speaking, from California and Mexico respectively. The former (the desert fan palm) is used for ornament in the Mediterranean, the latter (the Mexican fan palm) in California. *W. robusta* actually looks the less robust of the two, having a thin trunk that grows to an enormous height, but it is particularly resistant to salt. The old leaves of both hang down the stems and will remain for many years as a thick thatch that you can leave or have removed as you wish. Both grow fast if planted in well-draining soil and given plenty of water and fertilizer.

## Yucca
These desert and semi-desert evergreen sword-leaved plants are remarkable for their large heads of beautiful white or cream bell flowers; heavy and almost waxy in appearance, the flowers contrast with the tough, sometimes spine-tipped leaves. These leaves rise, in a rosette, either directly from the ground in the case of *YY. filamentosa, flaccida* and *recurva*, or from a branching treelike structure that may reach 8m/26ft. They are all excellent plants for giving substance to a cactus garden. There are variegated forms of *Y. aloifolia* and *Y. gloriosa*, and pink-flowered forms of *Y. filamentosa* such as 'Rosenglocke'. Perhaps the most spectacular yucca is *Y. whipplei*, which takes several years to reach flowering size and dies after setting seed.

## Yucca aloifolia
H 5m/16ft  S 2m/6ft  −7°C/19°F  d s c i
The Spanish bayonet is a slow-growing, normally upright but sometimes recumbent plant, with stiff leaves ending in sharp and dangerous spikes (it is a wise precaution to cut off the points with secateurs). It is picturesque when planted in clumps and bears its huge upright clusters of pale cream flowers in summer. Dead leaves can be removed to keep the plant tidy.

## Yucca elephantipes
H 8m/26ft  S 5m/16ft  −5°C/23°F  d s c i
The fast-growing spineless yucca forms magnificent, multi-branched clumps. The trunks swell at the point where they reach the earth, resembling an elephant's foot – hence the Latin specific name. The stiff aloelike leaves are larger than those of *Y. aloifolia* and not so sharp. The flowers are borne fairly freely in spring. Though this yucca will take drought, it does best with watering provided that the soil drainage is good.

# SHRUBS

It is possible to make an attractive, varied and easy-to-maintain garden based almost wholly on shrubs. While not everyone has the space for a tree – let alone several – most people have room to plant a number of small shrubs. And a shrub garden is, on the whole, much less labour-intensive than one based on perennials.

A high proportion of the shrubs suitable for a hot, dry climate flower in spring and rest in the taxing heat of summer. A number of them then bear attractively coloured fruits later in the year, and many are evergreen – so in spring, autumn and winter the shrub garden is never devoid of interest. If you want a lot of summer colour in such a garden, however, you will need to plant some annuals among the shrubs.

The root system of a shrub is not so extensive as that of a tree, and those shrubs that are not drought resistant are dependent on careful and fairly frequent watering. In a hot climate abundant watering tends to promote rapid, and often lanky, growth, so, to encourage short, woody growth and to maintain a compact, well-formed shrub, it is necessary to pinch out the growing points at frequent intervals.

Patio owners who have time for frequent watering will find that many shrubs grow well in big pots.

## Abelia × grandiflora
H 2.5m/8ft  S 3m/10ft  −9°C/16°F  o f 3

This very pretty small-leaved, semi-evergreen shrub is easy to grow and tolerant. The arching stems are strewn in summer and autumn with small, pale pink trumpets, and the reddish stars of the bracts continue to give colour on into the winter when the foliage is often shot with bronze. Suitable for sun or light shade, it needs occasional summer watering and makes a good small hedge, but, given fairly rich soil and good drainage, it will also do well in a pot. Prune after flowering by cut-ting out branches selectively, not by shearing, to preserve the graceful arching habit. The shrub is easily propagated by taking cuttings of the current year's wood in midsummer. The variegated variety 'Francis Mason' is not quite at home in full sun, and 'Edward Goucher' has rather pinker flowers.

## Acca sellowiana syn. Feijoa sellowiana
H 6m/20ft  S 6m/20ft  −7°C/19°F  d a c 2

This Brazilian evergreen, the pineapple guava, is useful and attractive in a number of ways. It forms, rather slowly, a large bush or small tree with small to medium sized grey-green leaves. In late spring it produces quantities of flowers with prominent red stamens and pinky-white edible petals. These are followed by quite palatable egg-shaped fruits, better in selected grafted plants, which should be eaten only after they have fallen. After flowering, the foliage can be hard pruned into any shape. It seems to thrive just as well in drought as it does in extreme moisture. Another great advantage is that it will thrive as a first line plant in coastal gardens. Even so, it is not one of the easiest plants to establish.

## Aloysia triphylla
H 2m/6ft  S 3m/10ft  −4°C/25°F  o f

The lemon verbena (occasionally still sold under the name *Lippia citriodora*) is a herby semi-evergreen shrub or very small stumpy tree of spreading, gangly growth, with long thin leaves that smell strongly of lemon. You can use these in cooking and cold drinks.

*Acca sellowiana*

*Choisya ternata* makes a fine evergreen bush with fragrant blossom

*Atriplex halimus*

**Aralia sieboldii** *see* **Fatsia japonica**

**Atriplex canescens**
H 2m/6ft S 2.5m/8ft −9°C/16°F d a c
The Californian saltbush is an evergreen shrub with silver or silver-grey foliage. As its common name suggests, it is salt resistant and makes an excellent first line of defence against salt winds and spray. *A. semibaccata*, the Australian saltbush, is lower growing, reaching about 300mm/12in, and makes a good ground-cover shrub under these conditions. *A. halimus*, the European saltbush, reaches about 1.5m/5ft in height, and like the other two is drought and fire resistant. Even if charred, it will sprout again. They grow better if watered occasionally and, for hedges, spaced 1.2m/4ft apart.

**Azaleas**
Many azaleas are planted in California and give good results in areas that have relatively high humidity in full summer. Plants, such as the Southern Indica hybrids including azalea 'Brilliant' and the 'Imperial' family, have been specially bred for heat resistance. These are not, however, widely available in Europe, and at the moment can be considered only as plants with which to experiment. Though indoor azaleas are popular winter and spring-flowering houseplants in Europe, outdoors they do not seem to survive for long. If you can provide

conditions azaleas like, that is, permanently damp but light, open organic acid soil under light shade, you may like to take up the challenge – otherwise you should be prepared for disappointment.

**Bamboo**
The light, airy, graceful form of bamboo looks extremely attractive around buildings and in courtyards – as a contrast to the heavy colour and substance of Italian cypress, holm oak and pines. The vertical striping of the bamboo stems and their light-green, fractured foliage will break up the monotony of paving, blank walls, and even the blind blue dome of the summer sky.

Bamboos can be moved when they are 4-5m/13-16ft tall to achieve an immediate effect, but make sure when buying large specimens that all the canes are green and holding their leaves. If the plants have been stored over-long or not adequately watered in the nursery they will rapidly begin to die back. When planted in a border or a container, bamboo plants must have generous and regular watering and feeding and may pose watering problems, particularly in midsummer, once established. Some of the stems may die in the winter cold but, when the spring comes, new sprouts, like giant asparagus, spring up from the roots; if no new green leaves appear on the old stems you can cut these down and use them for fishing rods or plant supports.

The most popular, and most commonly found, bamboos are *Phyllostachys aurea* and *P. nigra* with yellow and black stems respectively, and *Sasa palmata* with longer wider leaves springing from the stem like the fingers of a hand. All three do well in pots, given sufficient water, but planted in the open ground they are all very invasive, especially *S. palmata*. All are able to withstand far lower temperatures than they will ever encounter in a Mediterranean climate.

**Berberis**
There are over 500 barberry species and hybrids, many of which are tough enough to do well in dry hot gardens as well as being pretty in flower and fruit. The deciduous *B. thunbergii* and its red-leaved forms are the most commonly found. The two described below are especially useful fast-growing plants for all sites, including gardens situated on the coast.
**Berberis julianae**
H 2m/6ft S 1.5m/5ft −9°C/16°F d f c
This upright, semi-evergreen and very thorny bush has yellow flowers in early summer followed by black, blue-bloomed fruit and reddish autumn leaf colour. It is resistant to drought but the better for watering, and

*Berberis julianae*

*Brugmansia suaveolens*

makes an attractive and quite impenetrable hedge if the plants are spaced at intervals of 1m/3ft.

Berberis × *ottawensis* 'Superba' has a similar growth habit. With purplish-red foliage and red berries, it is a tough shrub, equally useful as a dense hedge.

### Brugmansia suaveolens syn. Datura suaveolens
H 3.5m/12ft s 2.5m/8ft −3°C/27°F m f
Brugmansias should be loved by discerning witches: they have large, pointed hairy leaves that look rather sinister. But their long, hanging trumpet-flowers are beautiful. Double or single at the mouth, and white in this species, they are prolifically borne and sweetly fragrant. However, the whole plant is very poisonous. Even if badly damaged by light frosts, the stump and woody branches will sprout again.

### Buddleia davidii
H 4m/13ft s 4m/13ft −9°C/16°F n f c 3
This semi-deciduous, rather open shrub is invaluable for achieving a quick brilliant effect. The first long flower spike on each branch is the largest, but smaller spikes from lower axils will flower subsequently, especially if dead flowers are removed. Added colour comes from the butterflies that this shrub will attract. Though drought resistant, it does better with a little water and can quickly be trained to form a standard. Unwanted

growth can be trimmed in autumn or you can cut back the branches in early spring as hard as you like, even to the ground to get the largest flowers. Cuttings root very easily. Various cultivars have been selected for their flower colour, such as 'Black Knight' (deep violet), 'Opéra' (heavy mauve flowers with a yellow eye) and 'White Profusion'. A new dwarf free-flowering race, including 'Nanho Petite Indigo' and 'Nanho Petite Plum', is excellent as a border plant or in wall side beds.

### Buxus microphylla japonica
H 1.5m/5ft s 1.5m/5ft −9°C/16°F o s
The common box, *B. sempervirens*, and its edging variety 'Suffruticosa', are not at home in hot dry areas so *B. microphylla japonica* should be used instead. This is slow growing but will make a good clipped hedge of any height from 200mm/8in to 1.5m/5ft, spaced at 250mm/10in intervals. It can also be used to make topiary shapes and can be grown in pots.

### Caesalpinia gilliesii
H 3m/10ft s 2m/6ft −9°C/16°F o s c 3
The 'Yellow Bird of Paradise' flower must have been christened thus by someone with a rich imagination. To those of a more prosaic turn of mind, the blossom is a clump of yellow leguminous pea-flowers with long red stamens. Even so, the effect is unusual and light, best

when seen against a dark background. The shrub is deciduous but produces neither flowers nor even leaves until the heat comes; it then flowers continuously.

## Callistemon

These very useful shrubs or small trees are rugged and resistant to heat and drought, though they grow best in moist earth. They like a light, deep, sandy soil and will take limestone – though the occasional dose of iron chelate is necessary, especially when young, as new growth is often particularly prone to chlorosis. Never remove the dead flower heads, since the new growth comes from the tip of the old flower.

### Callistemon citrinus

H 5m/16ft  S 4m/13ft  −6°C/21°F  o f c 2

This big, tough, easily grown species has spectacular scarlet bottlebrushes, 150mm/6in in length, borne mainly in early summer but sporadically the year round. The species is called 'citrinus' for the lemon fragrance of the leaf. *C. speciosus* makes a large bush with striking bright red bottlebrushes somewhat smaller than those of *C. citrinus*.

*Caesalpinia gilliesii*

## Camellia

If you like a challenge, try out your green fingers on a camellia. Few plants give such beautiful rewards. It needs a rich, acid, organic soil with leafmould or peat, and must be kept constantly moist. Protect it from low humidity, especially drying winds, and make sure it receives good light, though not direct sunlight.

Camellias make good plants for large containers where you can easily provide the acid soil they require. *Camellia sasanqua* varieties are most suited to the conditions and all will need additional iron chelate if the leaves begin to look yellow. Good cultivars include 'Bert Jones', 'Mine-no-yuki' (syn. 'White Doves'), 'Yuletide' and the hybrid 'Flower Girl'.

## Carpenteria californica

H 3m/10ft  S 3m/10ft  −6°C/21°F  o s c

Called the tree anemone in the United States, this very fine shrub is native to a small area of California. It is especially beautiful in midsummer, when white cistus-like flowers, with a central boss of golden anthers, cover the whole plant. At other times of year it is a serviceable evergreen. You can grow it from seed fairly easily, but the quality of the flowers will be variable, and it strikes quite well from cuttings. The plant does best in a spot that is not too hot or sunny – on a shaded bank or slope – and though it needs well-drained soil it should never be allowed to dry out. It is rather short lived and once planted must not be disturbed. The large-flowered 'Ladhams Variety' is said to be particularly striking.

## Cassia

The members of this large group of shrubs or small trees bear flowers in every shade of yellow but, with few exceptions, they are on the borderline of hardiness. The species discussed here are best for gardens that suffer from some degree of frost. All grow to about 1.5-2.5m/5-8ft and need occasional watering.

### Cassia alata

H 2m/6ft  S 3m/10ft  −2°C/28°F  o a c

This deciduous shrub is occasionally seen in coastal gardens. It has upright heads of quite large golden yellow flowers and an open, rather flat-topped shape. *C. artemisioides* will grow to 1.5m/5ft and makes a narrower plant. Its feathery grey-green evergreen foliage is covered with clouds of sulphur-yellow flowers in early spring. This shrub does best if kept rather dry. It is hardy to −6°C/21°F. *C. leptophylla* grows into a small spreading evergreen tree with large deep yellow flowers at the height of summer. It is frost-hardy down to −4°C/25°F. *C. marilandica*, which is hardier still (to

*Cupressus sempervirens* make a stately backdrop to ceanothus (centre) and viburnum (foreground)

−7°C/19°F), is a small pithy shrub that bears heads of yellow flowers with purple anthers in summer.

### Ceanothus

This outstanding genus of blue-flowered shrubs comes from California. They grow well in full sun and good drainage, need little water in summer and are good sea-side shrubs. Most flower in early spring and have a short life of five to ten years though they make up for this with rapid growth.

Ceanothus are fairly lime tolerant but frequently show signs of chlorosis and need dosing with iron chelate. Organic mulch, applied in moderation, helps to counteract soil alkalinity and provides all the food they need: do not give any other form of fertilizer. They dislike being pruned and usually will not re-sprout from old wood; occasionally large sections of shrub will die back. Remove dead wood in autumn or early winter; otherwise only trim lightly after flowering. Cuttings can be taken in late summer. Ceanothus species fall into two groups, evergreen and deciduous.

### Ceanothus arboreus 'Trewithen Blue'

H 5m/16ft  S 5m/16ft  −7°C/19°F  d f c 2

This is about the largest of the ceanothus genus and forms a small tree that is usually evergreen, though cold in late winter may thin it. The deep blue flowers, slightly scented, cover the tree in mid to late spring.

The other evergreens include *C. thyrsiflorus*, which will form a hardy small tree, while *C. thyrsiflorus repens* makes an excellent ground-cover shrub, spreading to 3m/10ft across and mounding to 1m/3ft high. There are many good American hybrids, including 'Yankee Point' and 'Puget Sound'. *C. griseus* is another good choice with large, mid-blue flowers.

### Ceanothus × delileanus

H 2m/6ft  S 4m/13ft  −9°C/16°F  d f c 2

The deciduous hybrids of the *C. × delileanus* parentage (and the closely related *C. × pallidus*) seem to lack the character and usefulness of the dark evergreen kinds. They have fine coloured flowers, but never seem to do so well, their foliage staying a light and slightly anaemic shade of green. 'Topaz' is a better darker blue than 'Gloire de Versailles' and *C. × pallidus* 'Marie Simon' has pink flowers. These and several other varieties are, nonetheless, worth trying.

### Ceratostigma willmottianum

H 1m/3ft  S 1m/3ft  −9°C/16°F  d f c 3

This is a deciduous drought-resistant shrub with bright blue flowers that is easy to grow. It needs cutting back to the ground each winter in frosty areas but in milder spots needs hard pruning in the spring to remove old wood and regenerate the young. *C. plumbaginoides* is a similar species but lower growing and more herbaceous in character, with a height of 350mm/14in and spread of 500mm/20in. The flowers are a deeper blue. Good on the coast and as a spreading ground cover, it needs to be cut to the ground every year.

## Cestrum

These frost-susceptible shrubs or small trees have no great distinction of form, but they bear fragrant tubular flowers for most of the year. They all need shady conditions, ample watering and feeding, and should be cut back hard after flowering.

### Cestrum 'Newellii'

H 3m/10ft S 3m/10ft −4°C/25°F m f c

This evergreen is probably the showiest cestrum variety. It displays deep scarlet-red tubular flowers continuously, except when inhibited by cold. It has dark green leaves and an attractive arching habit.

### Cestrum nocturnum

H 4m/13ft S 5m/16ft −4°C/25°F m f c

The 'lady of the night' is an evergreen, rather straggling shrub, with masses of small insignificant cream flowers. These have such a powerful fragrance that they are best kept on the outer edges, where they can tantalize rather than overpower. Cutting back the branches after the main flowering in early summer helps to produce a second flush and keeps the exuberant growth in check.

*Ceratostigma plumbaginoides*

## Choisya ternata

H 2.5m/8ft S 4m/13ft −9°C/16°F o f 2

The Mexican orange blossom is covered with white fragrant flowers, sometimes from late winter but usually from early spring and intermittently thereafter. Even when not in flower this neat, rounded, evergreen bush is attractive, with its shining, ornamental foliage. You may want to control its rapid growth by pruning after the main flowering. It must have well-drained soil and needs water occasionally but must not be over-watered. Planted at 1m/3ft intervals, it makes a 2m/6ft hedge.

## Cistus

Being totally drought resistant, cistus species are excellent evergreens for gardens that get no watering. They will grow in poor soil, including subsoils exposed by construction, and will help to prevent their erosion. They are hardy to −7°C/19°F and will tolerate coastal conditions.

Their foliage is often aromatic in strong sun, and they are charming in flower. For about one month in early summer they provide a succession of flowers, though each bloom lasts only for a day. Pinch out the longer growing points once the plant is half grown to encourage the flowering side shoots to form.

The most useful garden varieties might include *C.* × *cyprius* with large white flowers blotched with deep red at the base of each petal. It grows to 2m/6ft with a spread of 2.5m/8ft. *C. ladanifer* × *palhinhae* 'Pat' is a cross between two good garden species that makes a sturdy low bush (1m/3ft in height) with large white, crimson blotched flowers. Similar are 'Paladin' and 'Blanche', the latter without the blotches. *C.* × *purpureus* has light reddish purple flowers with a deep red blotch at the base of each petal.

## Convolvulus cneorum

H 1m/3ft S 1m/3ft −7°C/19°F d a c 3

Long, silky, grey-green leaves and very pale pink flowers throughout the summer make this small, dense evergreen shrub very pretty in a quiet way. It is an ideal plant for dry gardens, needing full sun, little water, good drainage and hard pruning if it gets untidy.

## Coronilla glauca

H 2.5m/8ft S 2.5m/8ft −8°C/17°F d f 2

This evergreen shrub will grow satisfactorily under all but the most extreme conditions of sun and drought. In the spring, it produces a superb display of bright yellow flowers. This species, with its silvery foliage, is more attractive than the otherwise similar *C. emerus*.

### Corynocarpus laevigata

H 10m/33ft S 8m/26ft −3°C/27°F d a c

If the aspidistra is the 'cast iron plant', this can surely claim to be the 'cast iron shrub'; for like the aspidistra it has a robust shade-tolerant constitution. The shiny, dark green, rather laurel-like leaves grow healthily even in passageways that receive no sun and the plant tolerates poor soil conditions provided that the ground does not dry out for long. It will flourish equally well in full sun and is happy growing in coastal areas where, in humid regions, it has been known to form a tree 10m/33ft tall. The flowers are not remarkable and the fruits are highly poisonous.

### Cotinus coggygria

H 5m/16ft S 9m/30ft −8°C/17°F d f

The deciduous smoke bush is so dubbed from the billowing clouds of purple-red flower heads that appear to float above the foliage from summer through to autumn. The leaves also turn marvellous shades of gold and red in the autumn. As it will grow without watering, gives the best effects in poor soil and is easy to grow, it is a prime candidate for a dry garden. The form 'Royal Purple' is a rather smaller but eye-catching shrub with reddish-purple 'smoke' and deep purple leaves throughout the year.

### Cotoneaster

On the whole most of the cotoneasters do well in hot, dry conditions, though whether these temperate zone plants are in keeping with the style of sunny gardens is another matter. They are moderately drought resistant but will grow much better if they are given some water from time to time during summer. Without this water the berries do not seem to develop well or abundantly.

All cotoneasters transplant badly so it is advisable to buy container-grown plants. With sympathetic pruning you can maintain the natural growth habit of a particular variety – whether arching, spreading, or clumping. *C. salicifolius* 'Repens' is a better spreader than *C.* 'Skogholm' which does not grow densely enough to choke out weeds and shows few berries.

One of the most popular species, for its arching form and good show of berries, is *C. lacteus*. This robust evergreen will reach a height of 2m/6ft and spread to 3m/10ft. *C. horizontalis*, another popular species, has tiny deciduous leaves and bright red berries on 'fishbone' branching. It makes an attractive fan-tracery effect that looks particularly good against a grey wall.

### Daphne odora

H 1.5m/5ft S 2.5m/8ft −7°C/19°F m a i

This marvellous evergreen shrub fully lives up to its

*Cestrum* 'Newellii'

*Coronilla glauca*

*Daphne odora*

*Echium fastuosum* contrasts with the red of an aloe

name and produces heads of very sweetly fragrant pink flowers in late winter. *D. odora leucantha* is the best. Most daphnes are small evergreen shrubs that produce fragrant flowers in late winter or spring. They all need good drainage and must always have moisture, though slight, for their roots. Try *D. aurantiaca, D. genkwa* or *D. bholua* if you can find them.

### Echium fastuosum

H 2m/6ft  S 3m/10ft  −5°C/23°F  d f c 2
This beautiful evergreen plant is half shrub half overgrown perennial. Long rough leaves stand out around the shoots to make a dense mass of foliage above which tower enormous multiple spikes of bright blue flowers. These conceal an internal structure of thick woody branches. An elegant shape can be maintained by cutting off spent flower heads and pruning lightly. As a quick supplier of mass it is unsurpassed. As a plant to give form and colour to rocky coastal situations with poor soil, it is ideal and it is one of the few subjects that will grow under pines. It needs only enough watering to get it going in the spring and can be neglected thereafter. In a word, it is the landscaper's dream!

However, since it does not like being held back in small pots – though recovering quickly when planted out – it is not always stocked by nurseries. In a larger pot it will quickly take up too much space. Plants grown from seed are rarely as brightly coloured as specimens propagated from cuttings taken from selected clones.

### Elaeagnus

These fragrant-flowered shrubs or small trees are relatively resistant to sun, drought, salt spray and wind. They grow fast in most soils, though they make the best show in poor sandy ones. They have unusual foliage thickly spattered with translucent brown or silver scales.

### Elaeagnus × ebbingei

H 3m/10ft  S 3m/10ft  −9°C/16°F  d f c
Though not much seen, this is one of the most useful big shrubs for dry, sunny gardens, being fast growing, evergreen and tolerant of most conditions. It is an excellent choice for a dense medium-height screen, or for a thick windbreak near the ocean. The leaves are silvery when young, later turning dark green above. Fragrant small flowers are produced in late autumn and the red fruit makes a good jam. The gold variegated form called 'Gilt Edge' does not seem to grow as strongly.

### Escallonia rubra macrantha

H 3m/10ft  S 4m/13ft  −8°C/17°F  d f c 3
This is probably the best variety of this evergreen genus for hot, dry conditions. The red flowers that appear in midsummer are larger than those of many escallonias

and its foliage is denser and darker. It grows best in a position that is shaded from the midday sun. All the escallonia species and their hybrids are of special value for forming a coastal hedge or windbreak.

## Euonymus japonica

H 3m/10ft  s 2m/6ft  −9°C/16°F  d a c

Many members of the euonymus genus need fairly humid conditions to survive, but *E. japonica*, the Japanese spindle tree, is resistant to drought and of great use for hedges or planting as a group. Its only drawback is that it is susceptible to scale insect, so you may have to spray it occasionally. A dense, upright, evergreen shrub, it will, with training, form a small tree up to 6m/20ft high.

Many varieties of *E. japonica* are available from nurseries. 'Albomarginatus' has grey-green leaves with a thin white edge, but the overall effect is dull grey-green. 'Aureus', (also sold as 'Gold Centre' and 'Luna'), has deep green leaf edges that make a striking contrast with the golden yellow centres. It needs continual attention because if you do not cut out branches that revert to green, these will develop vigorously at the expense of the variegated ones. 'Ovatus Aureus' (sometimes sold as 'Aureovariegatus') is the most satisfactory variegated clone, with an effect almost more golden than green and very little tendency to revert.

'Virginiana' is an excellent compact variety that makes a deep green, dense egg-shaped shrub 1m/3ft high. Planted 500mm/20in apart it makes a low hedge that needs almost no shearing. Placed at 1.2m/4ft intervals along a path, or around a pool, it makes an interesting series of formal shapes. 'Duc d'Anjou' is a strong clone with leaves mottled with green, grey-green and yellow to give a subdued but pleasing effect. 'Microphyllus' is a dwarf form with small leaves good for use as an edging plant in parterres.

## Fatsia japonica

H 3m/10ft  s 3m/10ft  −7°C/19°F  o f c 4

This is perhaps the most popular foliage plant for hot climates and is often still sold under the old name of *Aralia sieboldii*. It is excellent as an indoor pot plant or in a shaded spot out of doors. You can either cut it back in early autumn or late winter to make a dense large-leaved shrub, or let it straggle upwards for interesting trunk effects. Keep it well fed and give it some water in summer. In deep shade the leaves are dark green; in full sun they tend towards a sad yellow-brown, giving gradations in between. Midwinter brings huge panicles of small white flowers followed in late winter by purple

*Fremontodendron californicum*

berries that stain. Provided that you are prepared to clean up the fallen berries, *Fatsia japonica* is an excellent plant for growing in large pots on the terrace or around a swimming pool.

## Fremontodendron californicum

H 5m/16ft  s 6m/20ft  −4°C/25°F  d f c 2

This magnificent Californian plant is perfectly adapted to sun and drought. In spring it makes a large bush of brownish-green three-lobed leaves with large flat golden flowers that turn orange brown as they fade. But beware! It is summer dormant and should have no watering at all, apart from rainfall, between the end of spring and the beginning of autumn. If you do water in late spring or summer the plant will grow fast for a few weeks and then die as suddenly as if it had been given weedkiller.

'California Glory' is a cross between this species and *F. mexicanum*; it is better than either if you can find it, but is even more susceptible to summer watering.

## Fuchsia

This genus likes humid, temperate conditions, and although it makes a satisfactory pot plant, it is hard to find it a place in the garden where it will not go into decline, or worse, in the dry hot air of summer. If you have a shade house and can maintain the humidity in it during the hot months you may have some success, for the winter temperatures rarely drop low enough to harm it.

### Gardenia jasminoides
H 1.5m/5ft  S 2m/6ft  −6°C/21°F  m s 2

Both this species (Cape jasmine) and the similar *G. thunbergii* will grow into a large bush or small tree in a sheltered place provided that they get very little frost. They should be kept continually moist in a rich soil that is as acid as possible, though iron chelates will control any chlorosis. Grown in a big tub they flower indoors in winter when the creamy white camellialike blooms will fill the house with their fragrance.

### Genista
Most members of this large group of rather similar shrubs (some of which are thorn-free while others like the gorse are spiky) bear yellow pea-flowers in mid-summer. They will accept, even appreciate, dry rocky conditions and look well grouped on a bank; the low growers make good ground cover for dry spots.

The Mount Etna broom, *Genista aetnensis*, is rather later flowering than most and makes a fine specimen because of its large size and pendulous branches. It will reach a height of 8m/26ft with a spread of 6m/20ft. By way of complete contrast, *G. hispanica* forms fine, dense regularly shaped hummocks. This very prickly native of Spain is excellent for wild gardens.

### Genista monosperma syn. Retama monosperma
H 5m/16ft  S 4m/13ft  −8°C/17°F  d f c 1

This useful Spanish broom has milky-white fragrant flowers in early spring. The whiplike branches carry a feathery light arching fountain of fine grey-green threads in summer, and fleeting small leaves in winter. It prefers sandy soil but is not choosy and will, within a few years, make a diaphanous mass 3m/10ft or so high. Watering is unnecessary and it can be cut as you wish.

### Hebe
Most members of this genus come from New Zealand and find it difficult to tolerate drought and low humidity. Kept well-watered in sheltered shade, perhaps below a wall, many will make a fair showing. The frost-hardy garden hybrids based on *Hebe speciosa* are good coastal subjects, growing fairly fast to 1.5m/5ft high and wide.

### Hibiscus moscheutos
H 1.5m/5ft  S 1.5m/5ft  −7°C/19°F  o f 3

More of a perennial than a bush, since the stems die

*Hibiscus rosa-sinensis*

down during the winter, this is an astonishing plant with slightly concave plate-sized flowers (150mm/6in or more in diameter) in red, rose or white, usually with a small red centre. 'Southern Belle' is one of the largest varieties; 'Dixie Belle' is half the size but with flowers nearly as large. Both grow fast from seed and flower in the first year if sown in late winter. Though bought seed has usually been treated to speed germination it still needs a minimum temperature of 25°C/77°F. Once transplanted it needs heat and sun, food and water.

### Hibiscus rosa-sinensis
H 3m/10ft  S 3m/10ft  −2°C/28°F  m f c 3

This tropical evergreen shrub or small tree is only borderline hardy but is much appreciated for the huge, beautiful flowers, varied in form and colour, that it produces so abundantly during the hot season. Cultivated varieties differ considerably in size, leaf shape, manner of growth, resistance to cold and, of course, flower colour. In general you cannot expect any of these varieties to survive temperatures lower than −2°C/28°F and many will succumb in the lightest frost. Winter cold delays their development in early summer. Water generously during the warm season, but provide good drainage. Feed monthly and if there is any sign of chlorosis, dose the plant with iron chelate. Prompt action is required, since the growing season is short. It will do well on the coast if protected from strong sea winds.

*Hibiscus rosa-sinensis* hybrid

## Hibiscus syriacus

H 5m/16ft  s 5m/16ft  −9°C/16°F  o f 3

This deciduous shrub or small tree has summer flowers, up to 80mm/3in across, in shades of lavender blue, bluish reds, pink or white, single or double. It is easy to grow, does not demand much water and is resistant to frost. Good varieties include 'Oiseau Bleu' ('Blue Bird'), 'Hamabo' and 'Woodbridge'.

## Ilex

The holly, in general, prefers a rich, rather acid soil. With generous watering and some shade, a number of evergreen species make successful hedges and variegated bushes make interesting specimen plants. Since holly is unisexual a male pollinator is required to fertilize the female trees in order to produce the attractive berries that are one of the features of the genus. The roots resent damage, so use pot-grown plants carefully planted in early autumn and mulch around them rather than cultivate the soil to any great depth.

## Ilex × altaclerensis

H 6m/20ft  s 6m/20ft  −9°C/16°F  o a 4

This robust hybrid shrub or small tree has numerous varieties of which 'Golden King', with yellow edges to its leaves, is one of the more attractive.

Among the best hollies for dry climates are some compact, free-fruiting varieties developed in California from *I. cornuta*, such as 'Dazzler' and 'Burfordii'. In these the leaves are almost square in shape.

## Iochroma grandiflorum

H 2.5m/8ft  s 3m/10ft  −3°C/27°F  m f

Though tender and moisture loving this species merits planting for its fast growth and the clusters of hanging, purple, tubular flowers produced throughout summer and autumn. Cut back hard after flowering to encourage new growth. Look out for red spider mite.

## Jasminum humile

H 3m/10ft  s 3m/10ft  −7°C/19°F  o f 3

This fast-growing evergreen shrub or mounding climber has shiny yellow-green leaves of three to five leaflets and heads of small sweet smelling yellow flowers that bleach as they age. It can be trained and cut to form a long flowering informal hedge that needs only occasional watering. The variety called 'Revolutum' has more and larger flowers.

## Juniperus

There is such a wealth of marvellous junipers – each variety with its own foibles, each species with its distinct likes and dislikes – that an entire volume could be devoted to this genus alone. This section will simply sketch some settings for these horticultural gems.

The popular low-growing kinds look best when grown among rocks or on paving and encouraged to spread – though they may need a lot of space. Among this group are the *J. × media* varieties 'Pfitzeriana' (H2m/6ft s4m/13ft), a prickly pale green shrub for covering banks and untidy corners, and 'Pfitzeriana Glauca' (H1.5m/5ft s3m/10ft) a compact silvery-blue shrub that makes a good accent plant. If you lack the space to grow these, try the smaller, slower-growing 'Gold Coast' (H1m/3ft s2.5m/8ft), a juniper with feathery, bright gold foliage, or 'Mint Julep' (H 1.5m/5ft) a mint green shrub with a fountain form. A shrub that responds well to clipping into small topiary pieces is *J. chinensis* 'San Jose'.

Alternatively, if you want to cover a large area, *J. sabina* 'Tamariscifolia' (H500mm/20in s5m/16ft) is an excellent blue-green shrub that looks well. Other low-growing varieties include *J. sabina* 'Blue Danube' (H 600mm/24in s2m/6ft), with silvery blue-green foliage. Excellent for ruglike ground cover are the *J. horizontalis* varieties 'Wiltonii' (H150mm/6in s3m/10ft), which is a spectacular silver-blue colour, and 'Douglasii' (H 250mm/10in s3m/10ft), which has grey-blue foliage that turns purple in the cold.

For real drama try the rich, dark green *J. chinensis* 'Kaizuka' (syn. 'Torulosa' H5m/16ft s2.5m/8ft) a shrub with twisted growth that is much used in California. Other good upright junipers are *J. chinensis* 'Keteleeri' (H6m/20ft s4m/13ft), a fast-growing shrub of pyramidal form with small glaucous fruits, and J. × *media* 'Hetzii' (H 3m/10ft s4m/13ft), a dark green shrub that is both tall and spreading and is useful as a background to other plants.

Varieties of *J. squamata* and *J. communis* do not seem to do well under hot dry conditions.

## Kolkwitzia amabilis
H 3m/10ft s 3m/10ft −9°C/16°F o f c 2

The beauty bush is a graceful deciduous shrub covered with small pink yellow-throated flowers in late spring and later with pink bristly fruit. It is best planted in light shade and can be grown from seed though the resulting plants are not as good as those propagated from the cuttings of the varieties 'Rosea' or 'Pink Cloud'.

## Lantana hybrids
H 1m/3ft s 2m/6ft −1°C/30°F d a c 3

These plants, which are evergreen only if frost-free, are very popular in some regions for their continuous blooming in bright colours during summer and autumn. If there is a degree of winter frost they can be

*Lantana* hybrid

kept in check. In some hot climates, however, as in Australia, they can be highly invasive and are regarded, with their poisonous berries, as dangerous weeds. The individual flower heads are often rather garishly multi-coloured, but there is a good plain gold and a pretty white variety. They need only be watered if they are obviously suffering from drought, and not at all in winter.

## Lantana montevidensis
H 700mm/28in s 2m/6ft −4°C/25°F d a c

This trailing purple Lantana hybrid (syn. *L. selloviana* or *L. delicatissima*) excels as an easy and trouble-free ground cover for dry banks. If the soil dries out it becomes dormant but it will burst into leaf and flower again after watering. It puts down roots wherever it goes and clambers into shrubs and up trellises. If irrigated it becomes invasive, so do not plant it anywhere within reach of a sprinkler.

## Ligustrum

The privet is a genus with poisonous berries and greedy roots, but tough and useful for hedges or architectural bulk. Two evergreen privets are worth planting: the first *L. japonicum* is a very serviceable subject for hedges, topiary, background or substance anywhere in the garden, including those by the coast. It does best of all if given partial shade and will reach a height of 3m/10ft with a similar spread. 'Texanum' is the best form.

*L. lucidum* grows much larger, to a height of 9m/30ft and with a spread of 7m/23ft. It is often used as a tree, but can be kept small by cutting it into a substantial hedge or clipping it into a round bush. It is quick and easy-growing but the falling fruit are staining and the seeds sprout widely.

## Limoniastrum monopetalum
H 1.5m/5ft s 1.2m/4ft −6°C/21°F d s c 3

One of the very best first-line plants on the coast and useful everywhere, this shrub's tough, rather upright twisted, grey-green leaves taper towards the base. In summer it produces pale purple flowers. It is indifferent to poor soil, lack of water and sea gales and will take shearing into low hedges.

## Lippia citriodora *see* Aloysia triphylla

## Lycianthes rantonnetii syn. Solanum rantonnetii
H 2m/6ft s 2m/6ft −4°C/25°F n f 3

This rather loosely growing bush has lightweight foliage and small flat-faced pentagonal flowers of an intense purple-blue. It can be trained into a small standard tree, a wall climber or a round bush. Its long flowering season and healthy but controllable growth make it a popular choice for town gardens in California.

### Mahonia aquifolium

H 1m/3ft S 1m/3ft −9°C/16°F d a c 2

The Oregon grape is an excellent, suckering evergreen to grow under trees or in other dark problem places. The glossy prickly leaves have reddish tones. Heads of small, fragrant golden bells are produced in spring and are followed by blue-black edible fruits, much liked by birds. Reliable named cultivars include 'Apollo' and 'Smaragd'.

### Mahonia lomariifolia

H 4m/13ft S 2m/6ft −7°C/19°F d a c 1

This oriental relative of the Oregon grape is a magnificent, upright evergreen, with prickly leaves grouped densely at the ends of the vertical branches. It is useful for narrow shady places and looks well against a white wall that shows off its jagged form. Arching fragrant bundles of yellow flowers in cylindrical spikes are carried in winter at the tops of the 'canes', followed by blue-black berries which are popular with birds.

### Melaleuca

This Australian genus of shrubs or small trees will tolerate almost all adverse conditions. All bear bottle-brush flowers of various colours, and many make good subjects for dry gardens, though they are relatively little used in Europe. As they grow easily from seed, an opportunity exists for enthusiasts to experiment, choosing from among the 150 species. *M. linariifolia* does well in California where it is grown as a small tree with white flowers in summer and attractive peeling bark.

### Melianthus major

H 3m/10ft S 2m/6ft −4°C/25°F o f 2

This easy, fast-growing ornamental shrub is useful for creating interesting foliage effects. It has large, showy pinnate grey-green leaves and reddish flowers in early spring, and is obedient to pruning.

### Myoporum laetum

H 8m/27ft S 8m/27ft −5°C/23°F d f c

It is curious that although this plant is used in Mallorca for making a quick screen, its popularity in Europe does not seem to have spread very far beyond that island. Its small white flowers and purple fruits are not striking, but its speed of growth, ease of propagation, resistance to both drought and coastal conditions, acceptance of shearing, however severe, and its attractive dark green shiny foliage are qualities very much in its favour.

Myoporum is more highly regarded for hedging and screening in California where the cultivar 'Carsonii' is particularly favoured.

### Myrtus communis

H 3m/10ft S 3.5m/12ft −9°C/16°F d a c

This plant offers the dry-climate gardener the same range of possibilities as does the box in temperate climates. It is a neat, drought-resistant and largely heat-resistant evergreen that can be cut into hedges of almost any size, or left to make a dense large shrub or small tree. The small leaves are aromatic. The flowers, which appear in the spring, are followed by blue-black berries. A grey mould sometimes affects the foliage but otherwise the plant is very easy to grow, provided that the drainage is good and the watering frugal. It has been found in gardens for at least 2000 years, often cut into low hedges. There are a number of varieties, mostly hard to find, some with variegated leaves, such as *M. communis* 'Variegata', others naturally dwarf, such as *M. communis tarentina*.

### Nandina domestica

H 2.5m/8ft S 1.5m/5ft −9°C/16°F o s

The heavenly bamboo is an elegant evergreen clumping bamboolike shrub that is really a member of the

*Myrtus communis*

*Nerium oleander*

berberis family and which, like the berberis, has tinted foliage: the young growth is pink and red, and these colours return in the autumn and winter. Panicles of small white summer flowers produce red berries, more abundantly once several are established in clumps. It is drought resistant but much stronger with good watering. The chief enemy of this plant is cold wind and it is best sited against a sheltering wall. It also suffers from chlorosis easily but can be grown in acidic soil in containers and is a good houseplant if the light is sufficient.

## Nerium oleander
H 5m/16ft  S 4m/13ft  −7°C/19°F  d f c 3
This evergreen plant, together with hibiscus and bougainvillea, is the mainstay of dry climate gardening. Oleanders are often seen growing naturally in dry riverbeds where, in the beginning of summer, they can find underground water. This gives us a clue to their cultivation for they flower and grow best if planted in full sun, kept well watered until midsummer and, from then on, given only occasional watering. Left to grow naturally the oleander will form a multi-stemmed bush,

but it can easily be trained into a beautiful small tree that looks very attractive grown in tubs. It is said that it is better to pull up the suckers that arise from the base of any plants trained as trees, rather than to cut them off.

There are many named varieties, but the commonest are a double pink with white streaks in the flower, a shocking pink single, a dark red semi-double, a very pale pink with a red eye, a yellow ('Isle of Capri'), a pink buff that is a weak grower ('Carneum Flore Pleno' syn. 'Mrs Roeding'), and a white ('Album' syn. 'Soeur Agnes'). There is also a variety with leaves variegated with yellow, and with double pink flowers ('Splendens Foliis Variegatis'). The cultivars 'Calypso', 'Hardy Pink' and 'Hardy Red' may succeed in areas too cold for other varieties.

The only defect of this beautiful shrub is that all parts are very poisonous. Take care when burning branches or leaves not to inhale the smoke. You must look out for scale, a common insect pest on this plant. It is sometimes indicated by a sooty look to the leaves caused by fungus growing on the insects' excretions. Systemic insecticide is usually effective against this pest.

## Olearia

Plants of this genus consist of medium to large shrubs usually with white daisy flowers, sometimes blue, pink or purple. They come from New Zealand or southeastern Australia where humidity is relatively high. However, *O. × haastii*, *O.* 'Henry Travers', *O. semidentata*, and *O. traversii* all grow well, though flowering perhaps less, in full sun with moderate watering. Resistant to sea winds, they are useful in coastal gardens.

## Osmanthus delavayi

H 2.5m/8ft  S 3m/10ft  −9°C/16°F  o s 2

Related to the olive, this attractive evergreen shrub has neat, dark green leaves and white fragrant flowers in spring. It is a shrub of quality that can be pruned to shape, and will take, even prefer, some shade, but it is subject to chlorosis. *O. heterophyllus* 'Variegatus' is similar but with leaves like a variegated holly. It grows to 4m/13ft, with an equal spread, and is good for hedges.

## Perovskia atriplicifolia

H 1.2m/4ft  S 1.2m/4ft  −9°C/16°F  o f 3

This feathery grey-green shrub bears powdery blue flowers throughout the second half of the year. It is easily propagated by suckers and seedlings that appear around the plant, but if you have managed to find the improved variety 'Blue Spire' it would be better to keep to the suckers.

## Photinia serrulata

H 10m/33ft  S 8m/26ft  −9°C/16°F  o a 2

There are several hybrids and varieties of this evergreen species. All have great charm of form and glossy green leaves, which are coppery to bright red when young and sometimes scarlet in winter. They have large flat heads of white flowers in spring, followed by red berries. Varieties of the oriental species *P. glabra*, such as 'Rubens', and of the hybrid *P. × fraseri*, such as 'Indian Princess', 'Birmingham', 'Robusta' and 'Red Robin', are all brightly coloured and hardy. All need sun or light shade, moderate watering and a good soil, which can be alkaline. They can be pruned to whatever character you want in winter and can be kept down to a size that makes them useful even in a small garden.

## Pistacia lentiscus

H 4m/13ft  S 3m/10ft  −7°C/19°F  d a c

The mastic or lentisk, an evergreen shrub or small tree, is one of the most characteristic components of the *maquis*, the low-growing scrub that colonizes dry, uncultivated regions all over the Mediterranean. Though

*Pittosporum tobira*

it is, perhaps, not very exciting in appearance it has some excellent qualities that should not be overlooked. It is, of course, completely drought resistant and perfectly happy on the coast. It does not mind being sheared and makes an excellent hedge. The foliage has pretty red shades in the autumn, and the females have small red, then black, berries. For problem gardens, especially coastal ones, it is invaluable.

If you are turning the rough ground around your house into a garden, carefully preserve all the lentisks, feed and water them and cut them into hemispheres or other formal shapes. *P. terebinthus* is similar but twice the size of *P. lentiscus*. The pistachio nut comes from *P. vera* which is also easy to grow – but you need female plants of selected clones and a male pollinator.

## Pittosporum

Members of this useful genus of evergreen shrubs and small trees derive mainly from the antipodes. Most have fragrant flowers and almost all can be used to provide structure and mass. They are fairly drought resistant but look much better for occasional watering.

**Pittosporum tobira 'Variegatum'**
H 2m/6ft  S 2m/6ft  −7°C/19°F  o a c
This is quite an attractive plant and the dull silver foliage makes a good foil to the strong greens of cypress hedges. 'Variegatum' is less vigorous than the species and is good for sun or shade, but its colours are best in the sun where its leaves are smaller and its growth denser. Very occasionally a branch will revert to the green form and needs to be cut out, but generally it is of undemanding culture. The shrub has more character and may be more decorative when grown on its own roots, rather than as a graft.

The dwarf form of *P. tobira* grows slowly to 500mm/20in high, slightly more across, and is useful for edging, low hedges or small accents.

**Plumbago auriculata** syn. **Plumbago capensis**
H 4m/13ft  S 3m/10ft  −4°C/25°F  o f c 3
Well known for its bright, pale blue flowers, this rampant spreading shrub or scrabbling climber will quickly transform an ugly corner. Give it full sun and maximum warmth (it will freeze and be cut back to the ground even in light frosts). Water only enough to keep it growing well. It is easily grown, though variable from seed. A pure white variety is also available.

**Pyracantha**
H 3m/10ft  S 3m/10ft  −9°C/16°F  o a c 4
This is another genus that, like cotoneaster, does well on the whole but is difficult to combine with most dry climate plants. It looks best, perhaps, growing alone among rocks or trained up a wall.

'Mohave' is an outstanding cultivar and this, along with the 'Golden Charmer', 'Orange Charmer', 'Orange Glow', and the yellow 'Soleil d'Or' are the varieties most often available. They need less water than cotoneaster to fruit well but will do so more abundantly with an occasional soaking in late summer as the berries form. Some are subject to scab and fungal diseases, including fireblight, which can be controlled with a fungicidal spray in spring and early summer.

**Raphiolepis**
These high-quality, medium to low-stature evergreens

*Plumbago auriculata*

have dense, glossy green foliage and many uses, ranging from high ground cover or medium-sized hedges to accent plants. Furthermore they bear, according to variety, abundant white to dark pink flowers during the winter and early spring. New growth is often bronzy-red and the leaves may turn red before they fall. They are very popular in California where a large number of named clones is available. They never get out of hand and can be formed to shape by light pruning after flowering. At least occasional watering is needed. They are useful for second-line seashore planting.

### Raphiolepis indica
H 1.2m/4ft  S 1.5m/5ft  −7°C/19°F  n s c 1
A dozen or so varieties are worth planting, though many of these are hard to find outside California. The flower colour varies from white in 'Clara' to deep rose-red on 'Spring Rapture'. The blooms are followed by long-lasting blue berries.

### Raphiolepis × delacourii
H 2m/6ft  S 2m/6ft  −7°C/19°F  n s c 1
This hybrid of *R. indica*, raised in Cannes in the late 1800s, is better known in Europe and bears abundant smallish pink flowers.

### Romneya coulteri
H 2m/6ft  S 3m/10ft  −7°C/19°F  o a c 3
The California tree poppy is an ornamental semi-woody plant that can get out of hand, as indeed it has in California, but in Europe it is hard to establish. The foliage is silvery-blue and the large, crinkled poppylike flowers are satin-white with a central bunch of yellow stamens. Flowering begins in late spring and continues until after midsummer if the plant is watered. It does best in a warm sunny position in a well-drained soil of some depth. The roots should not be disturbed.

### Rosa
Generally speaking nearly all the enormous selection of roses now grown in gardens throughout the world will do well in hot dry climates. In such a climate, though, their normal resting period is summer and they can conveniently be pruned during this period. If, by irrigation, this resting period is denied them, the perpetual varieties will flower throughout the year and their lives will be correspondingly shorter.

### Rosa rugosa
H 2m/6ft  S 2m/6ft  −9°C/16°F  o f c 2
This species of rose forms a rounded deciduous shrub and is not used nearly as much as it should be considering its tough, coast-happy qualities and its enjoyment of sandy soil, which make it ideal for seaside

hedges and dividers. Some of the selected varieties are fragrant, some have double flowers of white through pink and red to purple; all have large red fruits.

### Rosmarinus officinalis
H 1m/3ft  S 1m/3ft  −8°C/17°F  d f 2
One of the best plants for newly created gardens, rosemary is a quick-growing evergreen, resistant to drought and fire, pretty in flower, aromatic and useful in the kitchen. In youth it is a compact and formal shrub, but this stage is relatively short and it soon becomes gnarled and straggling with age. Wild white forms are fairly frequently found but are not usually as strong as the blue nor as pretty. Various prostrate or weeping forms are also available.

### Russelia equisetiformis syn. Russelia juncea
H 1m/3ft  S 1m/3ft  −1°C/30°F  m a 2
This common houseplant is very easy to propagate and will grow out of doors provided that it is fed well, not allowed to dry out, and brought in if there is any risk of frost. It looks good in large containers and blooms

*Rosmarinus officinalis* (pink var.)

*Russelia equisetiformis*

*Tupidanthus calyptratus* (see **Schefflera arboricola**)

continuously, sending out small red tubular flowers on arching, rushlike, nearly leafless stems.

### Santolina chamaecyparissus
H 500mm/20in  S 1m/3ft  −9°C/16°F  d a c 3
The cotton lavender is a good, tough little silver-grey plant with a dense filigree appearance, bearing heads of yellow button flowers in summer. Although it covers the ground well and makes a good foil for other plants, it needs replacing every five years or so. The dense, compact form can be maintained by shearing the leaves. In its native western Mediterranean the flowers are dried and used to make *manzanilla* or 'camomile' tea. This is much stronger and more bitter than real camomile tea, which is made from the dried white daisy heads of *Chamaemelum nobile*.

### Schefflera arboricola syn. Heptapleurum arboricolum
H 6m/20ft  S 5m/16ft  −2°C/28°F  o a
The umbrella tree is a most satisfactory houseplant for, whatever its supposed preferences, it appears to thrive under almost any condition of neglect. In fact the schefflera is a candidate for more adventurous use. Said to like ample watering and humidity, it will do without much of either. Said to be tender, it will take slight, but not prolonged, frost. It prefers some shade but will take

full sun. There is now a wide range of varieties, some with variegated leaves and others of small-leaved compact form. Try the former to lighten up deep shade out of doors, the latter as a small foliage mass in the background. From the same family, and very similar in appearance, though less well-known, is *Tupidanthus calyptratus*, which makes a broader, denser shrub.

### Solanum rantonnetii *see* Lycianthes rantonnetii

### Sparmannia africana
H 5m/16ft  S 4m/13ft  −1°C/30°F  m f 1
This rather coarse, fleshy and hairy evergreen shrub can reach tree size but needs periodic rejuvenating by hard pruning. The house lime grows quickly to give bulk and winter flowers in a warm frost-free spot.

### Streptosolen jamesonii
H 1.5m/5ft  S 1.5m/5ft  −2°C/28°F  o f 3
This can be a very showy, light-bodied evergreen shrub of up to 1.5m/5ft or a straggling climber twice this height if trained up a wall or pergola. In either case, it is a pretty plant that is covered for much of the year with small but striking wide-flared trumpet flowers in yellow-orange and red-orange. Best in full sun, provided that it is watered occasionally, it is tender and will be cut by a frost, but reliably returns.

## Syringa

To bloom freely most lilacs need winter chilling to an extent that varies with the species and even with the varieties. The common lilac, *S. vulgaris*, is not really at home in warm climates, though the purple form is found in gardens where it will survive in shade and with generous watering, which it needs particularly in spring. Hybrids produced in California, such as *S. vulgaris* 'Angel White', 'Blue Skies' and 'Lavender Lady', have little or no winter chilling requirements, but are not generally available from nurseries in Europe.

### Syringa laciniata

H 2m/6ft  s 2m/6ft  −9°C/16°F  o a 2

The cut-leaf lilac is one of the prettiest shrubs for relatively mild winter climates. It has been cultivated in Iran for many hundreds of years, but there is some doubt about its origins and those of the very similar *S.* × *persica*; indeed the first is often sold as a variety of the second. The leaves of *S. laciniata* are deeply divided into many narrow segments as the name implies, while those of *S.* × *persica* are usually undivided. The fragrant lilac flowers appear freely at the ends of the branches in mid-spring, being darker in *S. laciniata* which is perhaps the better plant for gardens.

### Templetonia retusa

H 1.5m/5ft  s 2m/6ft  −5°C/23°F  d a c 1

Though short-lived this evergreen shrub loads itself in winter and early spring with deep coral-red pea-flowers that show up magnificently against the deep green foliage. Bushes can be trimmed to make a low hedge and the branches used for flower arrangements. The shrub will stand salt spray and sandy soil. Although it grows on calcareous ground in Australia, it may need iron chelate in very alkaline soils.

### Teucrium fruticans

H 2m/6ft  s 2m/6ft  −8°C/17°F  d f c

The tree germander is a useful grey-leaved shrub, naturally rather open in form but tolerant of shearing, which encourages it to assume a dense form. It does not need a rich soil or much watering and is good in coastal situations. The blue labiate flowers appear through most of the year and are of a stronger blue in the variety 'Azureum'.

### Viburnum

This is a very useful genus of garden shrubs, almost all of which are worth growing because of their tolerance to dry heat – though viburnums do best given adequate water and a rich soil.

*Teucrium fruticans* growing through *Laurus nobilis*

### Viburnum × carlcephalum

H 2.5m/8ft  s 2m/6ft  −9°C/16°F  o f 2

This hybrid produces large heads of white waxy fragrant flowers in late spring, and greyish deciduous leaves.

### Viburnum suspensum

H 2.5m/8ft  s 2.5m/8ft  −5°C/23°F  o a 1

In a quiet sophisticated way this is one of the most beautiful of all evergreens. Fragrance spills from small heads of white pink-tinged flowers in late winter and these become bright red berries by early summer. It grows well with a little shade and occasional watering.

### Viburnum tinus

H 2.5m/8ft  s 2m/6ft  −9°C/16°F  d f c 1

This very useful shrub (commonly known as laurustinus) will stand light or moderate shade but blooms best if planted in the sun. Flat heads of white fragrant flowers are carried all through winter, followed by purple berries. It makes a good hedge and cuttings from half-hardened wood, taken in summer, root easily.

The cultivar 'Lucidum' has leaves so large and glossy it looks almost like a laurel, matched by equally outsize heads of spring flowers. Better still is the variety *V. tinus hirtum*, which is absolutely resistant to full sun and drought, with a supposed origin in Algeria. *V. tinus* 'Eve Price', the pink and more compact variety, also does well and there are variegated forms.

# CLIMBERS

As they make their way upward, climbing plants use a variety of tricks to attach themselves to useful supports. Some plants, such as Virginia creeper, develop small sticky discs which they can fix to a flat surface. Others, including common ivy, anchor themselves by means of adventitious roots which they produce along the whole length of their stems. Planted at the bottom of a garden wall, these useful climbers will just shin up it by themselves. A warning, though – you may find it impossible to make any plant stick to a newly painted wall, because of the chemicals that are often added to the paint to prevent it going grey with mould or green with algae; these usually wear off after a year or two.

Plants such as wisteria, jasmine and sweet peas climb by twining around a vertical support, while bougainvilleas use both twining stems and hooked thorns to attach themselves. Other climbers cling by means of tendrils, or – in the case of clematis – leaf stalks.

Climbers are versatile plants, useful in many positions. With a sturdy support, such as a trellis, or a series of parallel wires stretched between uprights, many climbers make effective hedges and screens. Alternatively, given no support at all, a climber will trail, over the top of a wall, for example, or from a hanging basket. Allowed to trail along the ground, a climber such as ivy will form a weed-suppressing mat.

Many people are disturbed when they see one plant climbing up another – fearing, perhaps, that the climber may be killing its host. Certainly, the more vigorous climbers, such as wisteria, should not be allowed to climb up other plants. However, on the whole, little harm is done to the host plant provided that the growth of the guest is kept within bounds. Few sights can be more delightful than that of a frothy cascade of the small double white flowers of the Banksian rose, tumbling out of an old, dark, portly Italian cypress.

As a general rule, climbers like to have their roots in a cool, shaded position, such as that provided for them in the wild by the trees through which they climb. Few do well near the coast.

---

**Actinidia deliciosa** syn. **Actinidia chinensis hispida**
R 12m/40ft −9°C/16°F n f 2
This exuberant, deciduous, twining vine produces the fruit known as the kiwi or Chinese gooseberry, now very popular for its distinctive taste. The ornamental leaves are roundish, the size of a small plate, dark green above, grey below, and borne on reddish stems. It has fragrant, buff-cream, cup-shaped flowers in spring, and fruits develop later on the female plants. Plant a male for pollination; one is enough for several females. The female should be a graft of a specially selected kind if you want to eat the fruit. 'Hayward' is good. This variety needs some winter chilling to fruit well but temperatures lower than −7°C/19°F will probably kill it.

Actinidia needs good deep soil with plenty of food and water and full sun or only a little shade. It is excellent for covering a large pergola, which must be strongly made to bear the weight of its vigorous growth. The branches tangle easily, and the growing ends have a tendency to twine back upon themselves, so that unless you spend time training them, the whole plant soon begins to look like an outsize bird's nest.

**Asparagus**
Several members of this genus make useful perennial foliage plants that scramble over shrubs, trees and man-made structures using hooked thorns of various sizes. They will take full sun and some drought but are much happier in light shade in a moist, sandy, peat-enriched and well-fertilized soil, though even in these conditions they are not always easy to grow well.

Most asparagus have a bulky root system with numerous translucent ellipsoidal tubers. When these are planted in a pot, they tend to burst out in time. If the foliage is killed by a frost, the plant will sprout again from these tubers.

**Asparagus aethiopicus 'Sprengeri'**
R 2m/6ft −5°C/23°F n f c
Tufts of narrow leaves 20-30mm/1in long cover the arching stems of this attractive evergreen trailing perennial. Older plants bear pinkish fragrant flowers followed by red berries. If watered and fertilized it is a tough plant and less particular about soil than most. While many asparagus plants look pale in full sun, this one looks green enough to stand out.

Bougainvillea and plumbago (right) on a terrace wall in Ischia

Bougainvillea makes an attractive ground cover

*Bougainvillea* 'Apple Blossom'

### Asparagus setaceus

R 6m/20ft  −3°C/27°F  n a c

The fine fernlike foliage of the lace asparagus fern is the constant companion of carnations in bouquets and buttonholes. It is a good evergreen foliage climber that will produce a delicate airy effect against a white wall.

### Beaumontia grandiflora

R 10m/33ft  −2°C/28°F  n f 3

Large trumpet-shaped fragrant white flowers and lustrous dark green leaves make this a superb subject, very much worth growing. It needs good rich soil and generous watering. However, its use is limited by the fact that it succumbs to a few degrees of frost.

### Bignonia cherere *see* Distictis buccinatoria

### Bignonia violacea

R 5m/16ft  −6°C/21°F  o s 3

This neat evergreen (syn. *Clytostoma callistegioides*) has blue-purple flowers and glossy green leaves. It is rather slow-growing, but well worth the wait.

### Bougainvillea

R 15m/50ft  −3°C/27°F  d f c 3

If asked to make a shortlist of woody plants to plant in a garden around a villa, most people would include bou-

gainvillea. With its vivid, laserlike colours, strong growth – and total resistance to drought, ill-treatment and pests – it offers an easily obtainable, exotic effect.

The bougainvillea's natural habit is to climb into trees, though you seldom see it planted to do so in gardens. It can, for example, make a spectacular blotch of colour, scrambling up to spill through the leaves of a gloomy Italian cypress. Far more commonly it is used as a wall-covering where it will, in time, spread over a wide area and develop a thick trunk. But the spines, by which it secures itself in trees, are of no use to it on a bare wall and a system of wires and eyes, firmly plugged and screwed in, is essential. The natural growth of the plant is upwards, so make sure that the early growths are trained out sideways, low down on the wall.

You can also grow bougainvillea as a bush, by training it up a stake to the desired height before pegging down the arching branches to the ground. So formed it will make a huge mound which, with time, will reach 3m/10ft high and twice this across.

A colourful carpet of bougainvillea can be trained to clothe a dry bank. Plant it at 2m/6ft intervals and peg down the branches as they grow. Low-growing varieties suited to this use are available in the United States.

It is even possible to make an impenetrable barrier or a high hedge of bougainvillea by stretching high-tensile wire between strong supports and training plants to cover it. The structure must be really strong or a high wind will flatten it.

This altogether versatile plant was first collected in South America by the French botanist Philibert Commerson, who accompanied Baron Louis de Bougainville on his circumnavigation of the world in the mid-1700s. Since then it has found its way into almost all the tropical and warm temperate gardens of the world. Modern colour forms are hybrids and cover every shade in the red end of the spectrum, from rose to deep magenta, often with undertones of blue. *B.* × *buttiana* 'Mrs Butt' is a pure dark crimson, without any hint of blue; *B.* × *buttiana* 'Praetoria' is buff; *B.* × *buttiana* 'Alba' and *B. spectabilis* 'Alba plena' are whites; one variety – 'Mary Palmer' – has separate branches of magenta-rose and white flowers on the same plant.

*Bougainvillea glabra* 'Sanderiana' is one of the hardiest, though a rather violent shade of blue-purple. For attractive shades of pink, try either *B.* 'Apple Blossom' or 'Miss Manila'.

Since they are tropical plants, bougainvilleas do not do well in windy, exposed situations, and they will be damaged by frost. However, once established, the majority will recover from a frost.

Plants can be renewed annually by taking green cuttings in summer. In winter, woody cuttings will often strike, given strong bottom heat and rooting hormones. Planting should be done in summer, when the conditions are best for new growth. Take great care not to let the rootball disintegrate, as the plant hates root disturbance. Feed and water liberally during the hot months but give no food and no additional water in winter if it is growing out of doors and only occasional water indoors. Bougainvillea should grow rapidly at the rate of about 2m/6ft a year and, when it has almost reached the size that you want, you can cut down the food and water almost to zero. It is unlikely to die of drought once established. Prune as hard as you like in summer after flowering.

**Campsis × tagliabuana 'Madame Galen'**
R 7m/23ft  −8°C/17°F  o a 3
This is the least aggressive of the three campsis commonly found in nurseries. It is the elegant, if slightly showy, progeny of *C. radicans* and *C. grandiflora* and bears large trumpet-shaped flowers in orange-red. All the campsis species are, to an extent, self-adhesive, using aerial roots to attach themselves. 'Madame Galen' usually needs some help as its aerial roots are somewhat sparse. *C. radicans* has attractive red trumpet flowers but grows aggressively and produces many

*Campsis grandiflora*

suckers. The less exuberant *C. grandiflora* has slightly larger deep orange and red trumpet flowers.

All three provide effective cover for walls, fences and pergolas and flower in late summer. They grow best in full sun and should be pruned in early spring before new growth starts.

**Clematis**
R 3m/10ft  −9°C/16°F  m s
The climbing members of this genus live in scrub or low woodland, their roots in the cool shade of their competitors, their leaves and flowers lying about on top of them in the sun. Site them similarly in the garden with their roots in a cool moist place but with their heads in full sun – at the shaded base of a wall, for example, so that they can flower along the top and cascade down the sunny side. One of the best ways of growing them is exactly as they do in the wild, climbing over a shrub or small tree.

All clematis need well-drained but rich soil, so mix in peat and bonemeal before planting. If you are planting out a pot-grown seedling, set the roots deep, with the top of the pot-soil 100mm/4in below ground level. Keep the roots damp at all times, and feed well once established. Most deciduous kinds will look untidy during the winter.

Clematis fall into two categories: the large-flowered

hybrids, many derived from *C. viticella* and *C. lanuginosa*, and the different species. The hybrids have flat flowers in pure and intense colours, but are not easy to grow because it is difficult to ensure that they do not ever become hot and dry at the root. Among the more satisfactory are: 'Ernest Markham', a good red, 'Lord Nevill', deep blue, 'Nelly Moser', pale mauve with a central red-mauve stripe to each petal, and 'The President', midnight blue. All these hybrids can be pruned after flowering, and in early spring you can cut back to sound wood any stems that have died during winter.

### Clematis armandii
R 8m/26ft  −9°C/16°F  m f 2

This evergreen climber is worth planting for its foliage alone. The long, pendent, pointed green leaves show off large clusters of white flowers in early spring. If it is happy with the soil and situation it will be quite rampant, but is best if not pruned much.

### Clematis montana
R 7m/23ft  −9°C/16°F  m f 2

This vigorous deciduous climber flowers profusely in spring. The best varieties are the pale pink *C. montana rubens* and the deep pink 'Tetrarose'. They all tend to form a huge tangled mass, but the growth can be thinned heavily after flowering. They are all good for pergolas or bowers as well as for the tops of walls or in trees.

### Distictis buccinatoria
R 12m/40ft  −4°C/25°F  o f c 3

Otherwise known as *Phaedranthus buccinatorius* or as *Bignonia cherere*, this very quick-growing, robust and voluminous evergreen produces abundant trumpet flowers that open orange-red, with yellow throats, and mature to a purple-red. These inspired its common name, the blood trumpet. From late spring to late summer it is a spectacular climber with neat attractive foliage. It will climb walls without help; other supports must also be strong, for a light frame will collapse under the weight of its foliage. When young give it abundant food and water. When sufficiently grown reduce both and prune to keep it tidy.

### Doxantha unguis-cati *see* Macfadyena unguis-cati

### Ficus pumila
R 10m/33ft  −4°C/25°F  o f

This is a curious plant. Starting out as a delicate herringbone tracery of small roundish leaves, it may end by virtually engulfing a building in its 80mm/3in-elliptic adult leaves. This perennial evergreen is one of the most resistant to cold of the figs and one of the few self-clinging climbers, but it has enormously aggressive roots.

### Hedera
Ivy is one of nature's most useful plants, though many people look on it as a pernicious weed. This reliable, dense, tidy, deep-rooting, soil-binding, trouble-free, evergreen creeper roots as it goes and is self-adhesive on walls. It is ideal for draping eyesores and an attractive ground-cover plant. Excellent for binding banks against soil erosion, it will also make a hedge if grown on a trellis. However, it does need water in summer to look its best. Sheep and goats count it a delicacy and will strip a plant of leaves in a moment. Generally it does no harm to trees so long as it remains on the trunk and does not smother the leaves. However, it suppresses the growth of some trees hormonally and is particularly damaging to yew. Ivy will also keep a house warm and dry, if restricted to the walls, but it does lift roof tiles and needs cutting below the eaves to prevent this. It will also prise apart bricks if pointing is not in good order.

*Clematis armandii* 'Snowdrift'

In the juvenile stage, ivy climbs vigorously and has lobed 'ivy-shaped' leaves. On reaching the top of its support it matures and becomes fertile; the leaves are then almost unlobed, and small insignificant flowers are produced, followed by fruit. Cuttings of the fruiting adult forms will make round bushes that do not revert to the climbing form. There are many variants, though only four species are recognized by many authorities. The kinds most commonly found are discussed here.

### Hedera canariensis
R 20m/66ft  −9°C/16°F

IN *H.canariensis* 'Gloire de Marengo' the leaves are margined pale cream passing through grey-green to a dark green centre. The stems are purplish crimson.

### Hedera colchica
R 30m/98ft  −9°C/16°F  o f

The largest ivy, this has leaves up to 150mm/6in across and over 250mm/10in long. Three forms are common: 'Dentata', with small teeth to the tip of the leaf, is perhaps not as handsome as the plain species, which has larger, bolder leaves. Its variegated form 'Dentata Variegata' has yellow margins and a zone of grey-green between this and the darker green centre. 'Sulphur Heart' (syn. 'Paddy's Pride') has a yellow-green centre to the leaf. All are good as ground cover.

### Hedera helix
R 5m/16ft  −9°C/16°F  d a c

The common ivy is drought-proof and is available in numerous varieties from small pot plants to vigorous forms which may grow up to 30m/98ft tall. Many show attractive variegations: 'Goldheart' has a yellow centre.

## Hoya
R 4m/13ft  −3°C/27°F  n f 3

These outdoor wall plants or indoor pot plants have thick, fleshy, oblong leaves and clusters of heavily scented, star-shaped flowers that look as if they might be made of wax – hence the 'wax plant'. They need rich light soil and, out of doors, some shade – with ample watering whenever the soil dries. The flower clusters spring year after year from the same stubs. *H. carnosa* will twist its way up wire supports on a wall and indoors, in a bright window, it can be trained on cane or wire supports to form a ball. The variegated form is tender.

*Ficus pumila* (adult form) with a pink azalea

*Hedera canariensis*

*Jasminum polyanthum*

## Jasminum

This genus contains a number of species that will adapt to a dry, hot climate. All like full sun but will take light shade and all do better with regular watering.

### Jasminum azoricum

R 4m/13ft  −2°C/28°F  n f I

Either a dense evergreen climber or, under poor, dry conditions, a shrub, this jasmine has large white flowers in cymes that show up well against the dark, shiny green leaves, each composed of three leaflets.

### Jasminum mesnyi

R 3m/10ft  −5°C/23°F  o f I

The primrose jasmine is a dense evergreen arching scrambler with double or semi-double yellow flowers, without fragrance, produced sporadically throughout winter. It is best planted or trained high and allowed to cascade and should be thinned from the base after flowering. Supported by a fence, it makes a good hedge.

### Jasminum officinale affine

R 10m/33ft  −8°C/17°F  o f 3

This form of common jasmine, sometimes sold as *Jasminum* 'Grandiflorum', is a near-evergreen vine with large and marvellously fragrant white flowers, pinkish outside, borne from midsummer to winter. It is an excellent standby in the garden, whether it is allowed to climb over walls, buildings and trees, or made to pile up over a support to form a 'shrub'.

### Jasminum polyanthum

R 6m/20ft  −5°C/23°F  o f 2

A beautiful, vigorous, evergreen vine, this Chinese jasmine has a light airy form and bears panicles of very fragrant flowers, white inside, pink-purple on the outside and in bud. It is one of the best choices not only as a climber for walls, pergolas or containers but also as a ground cover, since the long growths will root along their entire length in light, leaf-mouldy earth. In warm places it will flower from the beginning of the year until midsummer.

### Macfadyena unguis-cati

R 12m/40ft  −9°C/16°F  d f 2

Also sold as *Doxantha unguis-cati*, the cat's claw, a more or less evergreen climber, is so well adapted to dry, hot climates that it seeds itself around rather too easily. However, for the right place it is invaluable, being one of the few really self-adhesive climbers and hanging on to almost any surface with tiny three-clawed tendrils. It is very fast-growing and brilliant in early summer when covered in sheets of golden trumpet flowers; these, alas, are soon over. A little mawkish, though tidy, for the rest of the year, it is an ideal covering for a high wall – or, for that matter, almost anything. The very large fleshy roots enable it to tide over any drought but they are greedy and hard to eradicate.

*Mandevilla splendens*

*Passiflora manicata*

## Mandevilla laxa syn. Mandevilla suaveolens
R 6m/20ft  −7°C/19°F  o f 3

The Chilean jasmine is an attractive, deciduous twining vine with very fragrant white trumpet flowers during summer and autumn, followed by pairs of long pods. Happy in full sun or light shade, it will spread naturally but the seedlings are variable.

## Mandevilla splendens syn. Dipladenia splendens
R 600mm/24in  −1°C/30°F  m a 3

This small twining evergreen climber has dark green oval leaves and rose-pink trumpet flowers all the summer. The colour is deeper in the shade. It is tender and will not survive winter out of doors anywhere that is susceptible to frost, but is a good subject for a pot or warm corner. After the flowers have fallen, let the soil dry out gradually and keep it rather dry all winter. When growing in summer the plant needs humid, damp conditions, rich soil and partial shade. Spray daily with tepid water if you can. Cuttings root easily and the plant can be grown on canes in a pot for house decoration. Even the smallest plants will bear flowers.

## Monstera deliciosa
R 3m/10ft  0°C/32°F  m a

The leaves of this Central American jungle climber are at first medium sized and entire. Ultimately they may grow over a metre (three feet) across and are elaborately perforated. The young form is often called *Philodendron pertusum*. Though a tropical plant it will accept winter cold down to freezing if protected from above − as it might be on a covered patio.

In the wild, its growth is largely aerial, and it thrusts its long, fleshy, wormlike roots into pockets of humus in dead branches and the crutches of live ones. So, plant it in a dark corner of a raised bed on a patio and, if you like, suspend perforated containers of peat up the wall for its roots to find. After a few years it will produce white spathe flowers and squashy fruit that hardly seems to justify the '*deliciosa*'. There are attractive variegated forms.

## Passiflora × alatocaerulea
R 8m/26ft  −6°C/21°F  o f

The edible passion fruit is produced by *P. edulis*, which needs a frost-free site, as does the spectacular red-flowered *P. manicata*. The best for normal use, as a cover for pergola shade areas, is the semi-evergreen *P. × alatocaerulea*, which is seldom without some flowers. *P. caerulea*, one of its parents, is nearly as good, though perhaps too strong-growing for small gardens. These two will grow well over trellises and other structures and can also be used as a bank cover. All need occasional water, and hard pruning to keep them from becoming a large tangled mess.

*Podranea ricasoliana*

## Phaedranthus buccinatorius *see* Distictis buccinatoria

## Podranea ricasoliana
R 10m/33ft  −4°C/25°F  o f 3
In the right conditions the pink trumpet vine, a popular deciduous climber, will cover wide areas. In autumn its long pithily woody growths come alive with pink, purple-streaked, open-mouthed trumpets in large loose heads. Light of weight, in the wild it will climb high and cascade down the outside of trees. Although it grows best with water and food during summer it then becomes very vigorous and hard to manage.

## Polygonum aubertii
R 6m/20ft  −9°C/16°F  o f c 3
Sometimes called the 'mile-a-minute vine' this vigorous, all-enveloping, more or less evergreen climber is covered in clouds of white flowers in autumn. In truth it is an untidy, messy plant that needs heavy pruning in winter, and can even be cut to the ground. It does, though, have its use as a rapid temporary cover. *P. baldschuanicum*, the Russian vine, is similar but deciduous, with slightly pink flowers.

## Rosa
Roses will grow very well almost anywhere outside the tropics. Indeed, in hot, dry climates they do so well and flower so profusely that they tend to have a shorter life, especially if not allowed to rest in summer. If deprived of water they will become dormant and summer deciduous, but they will break out into flower again in the autumn. Summer is thus best regarded as a resting season. The flowering season, which theoretically means all the rest of the year, can be regulated by hard pruning three months before you want it to flower.

## Rosa banksiae
R 8m/26ft  −7°C/19°F  d f c 2
One of the earliest climbing roses to come into flower, one of the most floriferous and one of the strongest growing, this thornless, fragrant evergreen rambler deserves a place in every large garden. It is found in four main forms: white or yellow, single or double. They will all form large straggling bushes left to themselves, but given support they will happily climb. The Banksian roses look superb tumbling in cascades out of dark trees such as Italian cypress, old carobs or holm oaks. All will grow without additional watering, are resistant to coastal conditions and are pest free. The cuttings root easily. Heavy pruning is resented.

## Rosa × fortuniana
R 8m/26ft  −7°C/19°F  d f c 2
Thought to be a hybrid between *R. banksiae* and *R. laevigata*, this excellent plant is in most respects a large-flowered form of the first of these parents and is just as vigorous. Its creamy, very double flowers are many times larger than those of *R. banksiae* and cover the arching pendent branches. It will grow well and hold its evergreen foliage without watering, and can be propagated easily and strongly from cuttings. It is equally good in coastal situations.

## Rosa 'Mermaid'
R 8m/26ft  −9°C/16°F  o f c 3
The pale yellow hybrid 'Mermaid' is probably more popular than its parent, *R. bracteata*, though rather harder to get going and less resistant to disease. Once it starts it will quickly form a large, more or less evergreen mound, or climb up houses or over rocks. Old examples have a trunk as thick as one's arm. The huge single flowers are pale yellow and appear continuously from midsummer to autumn, and fitfully during the winter.

## Rosa wichuraiana
R 6m/20ft  −9°C/16°F  o f c 3
This evergreen trailer has double white fragrant flowers and beautiful dark green shining foliage that stays fresh throughout the year. It has the useful habit of rooting as it goes, and, if allowed to sprawl about as a ground cover, will more or less swamp any weeds below. The tendency to flower intermittently, after the main display in midsummer, can be encouraged by giving water.

## Senecio mikanioides
R 6m/20ft  −5°C/23°F  d a c 2
This much-planted, semi-succulent evergreen climber flowers in winter with sprays of small daisylike flowers in a distinctly bilious shade of yellow. Although it can

get out of hand, the German ivy is valuable for its toughness and useful as a ground cover.

## Solanum jasminoides
R 5m/16ft  −4°C/25°F  o f 2

Related to the potato and tomato, the potato vine bears blue flowers in profusion in spring, and fitfully thereafter, but on not very distinguished semi-evergreen foliage. When selecting a specimen of the white variety from a nursery, look for a plant that is in flower so that you can be sure of getting a pure white rather than one of the pallid bluish-white mediates. Use it on pergolas or to tumble down a terrace wall.

## Tecomaria capensis
R 6m/20ft  −8°C/17°F  o a c 4

The versatile evergreen Cape honeysuckle bears brilliant scarlet flowers from early autumn to midwinter. It can be trained as a climber or as a bush, and will make a passable hedge or ground cover. It likes full sun but will suffer chlorosis on alkaline soils. This can be corrected by regular dosing with iron chelate.

## Thunbergia grandiflora
R 8m/26ft  0°C/32°F  d f 1

The Bengal clock vine is a wonderful climber, but not sufficiently hardy except for special spots. It strikes so

*Solanum jasminoides album* makes an attractive backdrop to a pot-grown bougainvillea

*Thunbergia grandiflora*

*Trachelospermum jasminoides* and a crimson hibiscus

easily, and grows so quickly, that you can almost treat it as an annual, preserving cuttings indoors during the cold months. It also sprouts well and quickly from the rootstock if all the above-ground growth has been frosted. The large pale-blue trumpet flowers are prolific and hang attractively from overhead supports.

## Trachelospermum jasminoides

R 6m/20ft −9°C/16°F o s 2

If you have some patience the star jasmine is a very useful plant: it has a steady evergreen permanence, neat growth, and fragrant white jasminelike flowers. It grows slowly at first, but then speeds up, eventually covering extensive areas. You can train it into a high climber or form it back into a bush, and it makes an excellent ground cover, flowering best in full sun.

## Vitis vinifera

R 20m/66ft −9°C/16°F d f 3

The grape vine is the best covering for a terrace pergola as it is deciduous and does not block the sun in winter; it is quick-growing and the attractive gnarled stems of older specimens look interesting when the leaves have dropped. If you buy a good variety it also gives delicious fruit. Against it you must count the need for pruning, training, and spraying, without which you will not get good grapes. Seek the advice of a local nursery to find out which varieties suit your locality.

## Wisteria sinensis

R 30m/98ft −9°C/16°F o f 2

The Chinese wisteria produces beautiful long racemes of blue or white flowers, and grows perfectly well in hot, dry climates, although it has the reputation of being difficult to get going. Feed and water young plants generously, but be rather mean once they are established. How much to water is a matter of judgment, but the plant dislikes being too dry at the roots and an occasional thorough watering, even of old plants, is advisable. At all stages this deciduous vine tends to suffer from chlorosis; the best way of dealing with this is to apply iron chelate as soon as you notice the young growths becoming pale.

The plant grows by means of long whippy new shoots, but flowers on short lateral spurs. Regulate the former to obtain the structure that you want, and cut all superfluous growth back in winter to the flower buds at the base of the spurs, which are evident from their fatness. During the summer you can also cut back all unwanted young growth. This pruning and trimming is needed to prevent the vine from becoming a huge tangled mass of intertwining stems with few flowers. You should propagate by means of layering, since seedlings take years to flower and grafts send up suckers. Eventually, if all goes well, your problem will be to provide sufficient support for what can become, in size, almost a sprawling tree.

# PERENNIALS

The perennials considered here are those adapted to Mediterranean conditions and are taken to mean plants that do not usually become woody at the base, but that have a normal life span of at least three years. Many die to the ground every year during winter, and these tend to be hardier than those that are evergreen.

The division between annuals and perennials is not finely drawn. Many plants grown as 'annuals' in regions with prolonged frosts will overwinter and live for several years in milder climates – some stocks, for instance, may grow, in time, into shrubs with thick, woody trunks. Other plants, looked on as perennials in colder climates, will not stand very hot, dry summers and are best treated as annuals – polyanthus is an example. Yet others set seed so freely that they reappear reliably every year, and can thus be treated as perennials.

Perennials are useful both for planting in the open ground and for growing in containers. There are many handsome perennials that are disease free, do not need frequent division or replacement, and will swamp competition from weeds: they make excellent trouble-free ground cover. For growing in pots, choose plants that have attractive foliage and habit, a long flowering season, and a robust constitution.

Of the perennials that form clumps, many die down in winter when the spent foliage has been cut to the ground. Every two or three years the clumps should be dug up, divided and replanted (the centre of the clump often has to be discarded). This treatment should be carried out in early autumn in the case of spring-flowering perennials and in early spring (just as growth begins) for those that flower in summer or autumn.

A mixed border of shrubs interplanted with flowering perennials

*Acanthus spinosus*

## Acanthus
H 1.2m/4ft S 1m/3ft −9°C/16°F o f 1

Considered to be one of the finest foliage plants for the shrub border, acanthus should be used with caution for it can easily become a pest – though admittedly a handsome and classical one. Since the explosive pods scatter seed over a wide area and it will regrow from any scrap of root, the plant is hard to eradicate, but it is tough, good for odd rough corners and places where the re-seeding can be contained as well as under trees, where not much else will grow. It is used with great effect in Mexico City around the boles of trees that have been ringed by low retaining walls. There, though the trees may be dying because of smog, the acanthus flourishes.

It is very ornamental in winter and spectacular in spring, but the summer drought and the effort of seeding wilt it, so that a tidying-up operation is needed in midsummer and, once the spent leaves and stems have been cut back, the site remains bare until autumn. *A. mollis*, with its spires of purplish white flowers, is the one most commonly found and covers the ground well. *A. spinosus* is similar but has beautiful, deeply cut leaves.

## Ajuga reptans
H 100mm/4in S 1m/3ft −8°C/17°F n f

A useful ground cover for sun or light shade, *A. reptans* spreads rapidly by runners and throws up 200mm/8in-spikes of blue flowers from late winter to early summer. The rosettes of leaves vary both in size and in colour in a wide range of cultivated varieties. *A. reptans* itself has dark green leaves while 'Atropurpurea' has leaves with deep purple-bronze tones and 'Burgundy Glow' has added cream and pink. They will take full sun, which helps to bring out the best colours, but they grow best with some shade and regular watering, as well as occasional feeding, though not in midsummer. To tidy up a patch of ajuga, use a lawnmower with the blades set high.

## Arctotheca calendula
H 100mm/4in S 600mm/24in −4°C/25°F o f c 2

The Cape weed is an invasive evergreen with yellow daisy flowers, 50mm/2in across, held above semi-prostrate, grey-green leaves. Best kept out of the garden, it is a useful ground cover for difficult terrains, such as exposed subsoil banks, and coastal extremities.

## Arctotis
H 600mm/24in S 800mm/32in −7°C/19°F d a c 1

The spring-flowering African daisies need water only when they are growing, in winter. Arctotis hybrids, which include those once known as × Venidio-arctotis hybrids, are shortlived perennials that come in an assortment of yellows, white tinged with purple, red-orange, and purple, all with a dark centre, held on long stalks well above the clump of grey-green foliage that grows to 250mm/10in. *A. acaulis* is a similar, but lower growing, spreading perennial with yellow dark-eyed flowers that make a good show in early spring.

## Arundo donax
H 8m/26ft S 1m/3ft −7°C/19°F m f c

This common reed grows wild in wet places in many tropical and temperate regions. The whitish plumes of flowers are attractive but it is extremely invasive and messy, best kept out of the smaller garden and treated with care in the large one. Every winter the canes can be cut to the ground and used to support beans and perennials, though they do not compare in strength with those of the bamboo. Frost will brown the foliage but the roots are resistant. It prefers rich, wet conditions but will survive short drought and will grow in ordinary soil if well watered.

## Aspidistra elatior syn. Aspidistra lurida
H 750mm/30in S 250mm/10in −4°C/25°F o s

The aspidistra is a fine foliage plant and so long-suffering that it usually gets maltreated. It is better adapted than virtually any other plant to low light levels but is happiest in light shade and a rich, moist, porous organic soil. With this treatment it is quite at home out of doors and its dark lance-shaped leaves, which have a hard rustling feel, will grow more than 600mm/24in long. Although the aspidistra is resilient, it is also slow growing, may be hard to find and is expensive.

## Asplenium bulbiferum

H 1m/3ft  S 1.2m/4ft  −2°C/28°F  m a

This beautiful fern has fine, filigree fronds and grows well in light uncompacted soil given moisture and fairly heavy shade. Small plantlets on the fronds make new plants when they fall to the ground and take root. It may be slow to reach its final size and full beauty.

## Aster

Four groups of asters − *A. amellus*, *A.* × *frikartii*, *A. novae-angliae* and *A. novi-belgii* (the Michaelmas daisy) − all make excellent border plants for late summer. They will grow in ordinary soil in sun and only need occasional watering. They vary in height from 150mm/6in to 2m/6ft, the larger sizes being suitable for planting among shrubs or in borders and the smaller ones as edging and in containers. They are resistant to most pests and are trouble free. Every two years dig up the clumps, in early spring, and replant sections of strong new growth from the periphery, discarding the old central roots. All are hardy to −9°C/16°F.

## Aubrieta

H 150mm/6in  s 600mm/24in  −9°C/16°F  o a 2

Easily grown from seed, aubrieta forms a spreading mound of blue, purple or red when it flowers in the early spring. It is a practical plant for rockeries and chinks in walls and pavements, provided that the rains are good in the winter and that it has occasional watering in summer. Light shade helps too. After flowering, plants will look sad through to the end of autumn but their appearance can be improved by shearing off the dead blooms. This also prevents the aubrieta from seeding − the self-sown seedlings usually being of poor quality.

## Begonia

One of the keys to the successful cultivation of begonias is to maintain high atmospheric humidity, which means that this group is not very well adapted to outdoor use in regions where, in summer, the air is very dry. However the modern fibrous-rooted F1 *B. semperflorens* varieties, which come in low (250mm/10in) or intermediate (to

*Arundo donax*

450mm/18in) sizes, do well in peat-enriched soil with ample watering even in full sun − though they are happier in shade. They flower throughout the year and last many years. The intermediate kinds are, on the whole, better for gardens; the low size for pots. They suffer badly even at −2°C/28°F. Do not be afraid to chop them back if they become leggy. Flowers are found in shades of red through pink to white, while one variety has red edges on white petals; the leaves come in bright green or bronze, which stands the sun rather better.

The largest rhizomatous begonia is *B. hederifolia*, a very ornamental plant for indoors or out, that may have leaves up to 450mm/18in across on thick stalks, 40mm/1.5in in diameter and 600mm/24in long. The flowers are light pink in large dispersed heads 1.2m/4ft high and the leaves are usually a curious, blotchy, dark brownish green. Planted out of doors, it will lose its leaves in winter but quickly sprouts back in spring if grown in a sheltered site.

## Bergenia crassifolia

H 300mm/12in  S 1m/3ft  −9°C/16°F  m s c 1

The ornamental, winter-blooming *B. crassifolia* has large, round, evergreen leaves and heads of flowers in various tones of pink, rose and purple, held well above the semi-prostrate foliage. This perennial would be far more popular if it did not need shade and damp to flower well – it makes an excellent ground cover if you can supply these conditions. The hybrids come in a wider range of colours, including white.

## Campanula

Most of these blue bell flowers like moisture and shade and lack vigour in a hot, dry climate. *C. portenschlagiana*, however, is more robust and makes an attractive 150mm/6in-high ground cover in light shade, bearing masses of deep blue flowers during the summer. It will withstand winter temperatures to −9°C/16°F.

## Centranthus ruber

H 1m/3ft   S 1m/3ft   −9°C/16°F   d a

The valerian is greatly under-rated and ideal for dry gardens where it will give a colourful show over many months and come back every year with increasing effect. It can be found in red, pink and white, and will self-seed fairly freely unless the old flower heads are cut off.

## Cerastium tomentosum

H 150mm/6in   S 600mm/24in   −9°C/16°F   d a 2

This low, creeping perennial has silver-grey foliage, and is completely covered in white flowers in early summer. Grouped with other rockery plants it makes an excellent foil. The best cultivar is 'Yo Yo'.

## Chrysanthemum now Dendranthema

In many parts of Europe the hybrid cultivars known as florists' chrysanthemums have long been associated with the dead and are in great demand for All Saints Day to decorate graves. The use of chrysanthemums as an all-year-round pot plant is, however, becoming more widespread. Dwarf varieties are beginning to gain the reputation as houseplants that they so well deserve, and dwarf mounding hybrids such as 'Autumn Glory' are beginning to be accepted as excellent perennial bedding plants. Apart from these hybrids there are several good species.

## Argyranthemum frutescens syn. Chrysanthemum frutescens

H 1.5m/5ft   S 3m/10ft   −5°C/23°F   o f c 2

Marguerites or Paris daisies are used extensively in gardens and are fairly tolerant of drought, though you will not be proud of them unless they receive an occasional soaking. They like full sun and are excellent for coastal use. *A. frutescens* itself is a large-bodied, large-flowered form, while *A. frutescens foeniculaceum* has feathery, glaucous leaves and smaller white flowers. Yellow forms include the Boston yellow daisy, *A.* 'Chrysaster' and the larger-flowered 'Jamaica Primrose'. There is a pale pink ('Mary Wootton') and a mid-pink ('Vancouver') with double centres.

All are quick growing and the large white will make a globe more than 1m/3ft in diameter by late summer from a small specimen planted out in early spring. Do not prune them back into hard wood as this seldom produces new shoots; frequent trimming is better, with complete renewal of the plant from cuttings every three or four years.

The white-flowered species make good standards, but the coloured hybrids tend to be rather too lax for this treatment.

Pink *Centranthus ruber* amid *Spartium junceum*

*Argyranthemum frutescens*

**Leucanthemum × superbum** syn. **Chrysanthemum maximum** of gardens
H 750mm/30in S 1m/3ft −9°C/16°F m a c 2
The Shasta daisy needs moisture, rich soil and light shade to produce an almost continuous display of single white, yellow-centred daisy flowers.

**Coreopsis verticillata**
H 500mm/20in S 400mm/16in −9°C/16°F o f c 3
This commendable garden plant is easily grown from seed, drought resistant and rugged. The flowers, borne from midsummer to autumn, are bright yellow in 'Early Sunrise' and pale yellow in 'Moonbeam'. Flowering will continue if the faded heads are removed.

**Cortaderia selloana**
H 4m/13ft S 2m/6ft −9°C/16°F d f c 4
Pampas grass is very fast growing and resistant to most adverse conditions – wind, salt, humidity, drought and poor earth, whether acid or alkaline – though it has a preference for light, sandy soil. Strains exist in various sizes, and the largest may grow to a height of 5m/16ft if watered, becoming too big for small gardens. The plumes emerge in late summer in various shades; 'Monstrosa' and 'Sunningdale Silver' produce fine large plumes of silver-white; 'Rendatleri' is a grubby pink fading to grey. This is not a plant to grow near swimming pools because of the dangerously sharp leaf edges. Burn off old foliage every spring.

**Cynara scolymus**
H 1m/3ft S 600mm/24in −9°C/16°F o f 2
The globe artichoke is worth considering as a garden plant for it is drought resistant and can supply attractive silver height and bulk at the back of a border. The cardoon is similar with more deeply divided leaves which may be prickly. Both can become very untidy in summer, especially if not watered. Globe artichoke flowers can be eaten in bud or left as ornament; blue and sweetly scented, they are attractive to butterflies. Plant only selected, named varieties if you want to eat the buds.

**Dianthus**
This is a very popular genus and deservedly so. Many species have a distinction of form that has made them popular as cut flowers and the carnation, of course, is a favourite buttonhole bloom. They will grow in a poor, dry soil if there is moisture below, or in holes in any wall that has a damp backing; they most like a moderately watered, organically rich soil that drains well.

Normally dianthus species grow in clumps of grassy leaves, but in time, the clump loses its identity and becomes a straggling patch of woody stems. Many – especially the larger-flowered double types such as the carnations – benefit from frequent renewal from the easily rooted cuttings.

**Dianthus barbatus**
H 600mm/24in S 600mm/24in −9°C/16°F o f
Sweet William is an easily grown, showy biennial, available in a wide range of bright colours. A few varieties flower the first year from seed, but less copiously.

**Dianthus caryophyllus**
H 800mm/32in S 300mm/12in −9°C/16°F o a 3
Carnations take many forms. The tallest, such as the 'Sim' varieties, are grown for cutting. These all need the support of canes, but are quite satisfactorily grown in the border or in pots. Much of the work involved in tying up is avoided with the dwarf varieties, such as 'Dwarf Fragrance' and the 'Knights'; these produce quantities of fully double flowers in the same great range of colours as the cutting carnations. There are also showy border carnations, propagated by cuttings, that have been selected for scent and flower colour.

**Dianthus deltoides**
H 250mm/10in S 500mm/20in −9°C/16°F o a 3
The maiden pink has a low, creeping habit. One of the best forms, 'Brilliant' is deep crimson and very long-flowering. Slightly taller and with an upright habit, *D. gratianopolitanus* (syn. *D. caesius*) is a miniature pink with tufted, often rather silver, foliage and single flowers in various shades of pink and red. *D. plumarius*, the common pink, is robust, with attractive frilly edged petals and will grow to 350mm/14in with a spread of 500mm/20in.

**Erigeron karvinskianus**
H 350mm/14in S 500mm/20in −5°C/23°F o a c
This plant may also be sold as *Vittadinia* or *Erigeron* 'Profusion', 'Mexican Daisy' or, incorrectly, 'Spanish Daisy'. Though at first sight it appears far too light and frail to be a nuisance, it is tough and verges on being a weed. Bearing a profusion of small daisylike flowers, white with a touch of pink, for most of the summer, it will accept drought, heat, root competition, some frost and poor soil. It naturalizes well, self-seeding and creeping over wide areas if not restrained. As well as making a good ground cover it can be used in hanging baskets and around the base of trees in big pots, and it will hang down terrace walls if planted along the top. Erigeron will stand some shade and grows faster and looks better for watering.

*Felicia amelloides*

## Euphorbia pulcherrima

H 3m/10ft  S 3m/10ft  −1°C/30°F  o f I

The poinsettia, with its vivid scarlet and green leaves, has now become almost as much of a symbol of Christmas as the holly. The plant originates from Mexico, where it grows to great heights in the wild, but numerous sports have been selected and propagated, including the pot plants so popular for midwinter festivities, often no more than 400mm/16in in height.

The colourful leafy bracts may remain on the plant for up to three months. Scarlet is the commonest colour, but varieties with pink or white bracts are often seen, while still others are red with pink blotching and speckling. All these varieties are naturally branching and robust, so that each plant has a number of self-supporting heads. The poinsettia likes high light intensities and grows rapidly in full sun at temperatures above 25°C/77°F. Once it has produced its coloured bracts, it will be quite happy at 10°C/50°F or less and will accept much lower lighting levels. It also likes low humidity but is sensitive to atmospheric pollution.

During the growing season the poinsettia needs heavy feeding but should not be fertilized during the branch formation period. The plant asks for no more than moderate watering whenever the foliage begins to droop slightly. In frost-free areas it can be planted out in the garden permanently; otherwise grow it as a pot plant, or plant it out for the summer and dig it up again when the temperature drops, repotting in fresh soil. Indoors, poinsettia must continue to have full light during the day and total darkness at night, uninterrupted by any artificial light, if you want the coloured bracts to 'flower'. Throughout the growing season, pinch out the growing tips, once they exceed 300mm/12in in length, to give compact plants covered in flowers.

## Euryops pectinatus

H 1.5m/5ft  S 1.2m/4ft  −3°C/27°F  o a c I

This shrubby perennial is popular in California but under-appreciated elsewhere. The attractive foliage is enlivened from autumn to spring by a display of yellow daisylike flowers held well above the leaves. It is naturally tidy and can be pruned during the midsummer dormant period, when it requires very little water. Given well-drained soil it is easy-going and makes a valuable garden plant, useful for coastal sites.

## Felicia amelloides syn. Agathea coelestis

H 500mm/20in  S 1.5m/5ft  −5°C/23°F  n f c 2

The blue marguerite is a popular plant, useful as a ground cover or for the front of the border. The foliage forms a mound, which is decked with small, pale blue daisylike flowers, with yellow centres. These appear as soon as the temperature begins to rise in spring and flowering continues, though less profusely, throughout the year. It needs some watering, but not so much that it begins to look untidy with uncontrolled growth; trim at any time to stop this and cut back hard, if necessary, in autumn to maintain a good shape.

## Gaillardia × grandiflora 'Goblin'

H 450mm/18in  S 450mm/18in  −9°C/16°F  n a c

This compact plant flowers continuously from late spring to autumn and will even bloom all year round, given occasional watering and the absence of frost. The blanket flower's daisylike blooms are very showy red, edged yellow, with a dark centre.

## Gazanias

These splendid plants, with their dazzling daisylike flowers, come in two types. The hybrids, of complex parentage, are usually called G. × *hybrida* and grow to 250mm/10in tall with a similar spread. They bear gaudily striped flowers, with iridescent centres, held well above the tufted mound of foliage. The creeping types, based on G. *rigens*, grow to 150mm/6in but spread to 700mm/28in and have silvery foliage and smaller white, yellow, double yellow or orange flowers.

*Leonotis leonurus*

leaves. 'Hidcote' has a very dark violet flower but is not as robust. The Mediterranean native *L. stoechas* (French lavender) remains healthy under most conditions and will make a good small hedge. Dead lavender heads can be trimmed off in autumn, but leave any heavy pruning to the spring.

### Leonotis leonurus
H 2m/6ft  s 1.5m/5ft  −6°C/21°F  o f 3
Leonotis makes up for being a little coarse in form with an eye-catching display of orange tubular flowers, 50mm/2in long, borne in whorls at every node along the stem. At its best, it can be very attractive – but this depends on giving it a hot position, full sun, occasional watering and trimming it lightly to shape after the spring and autumn flowerings.

### Limonium perezii
H 750mm/30in  s 600m/24in  −3°C/27°F  o a c
This sea lavender grows wild on salty foreshores but is admirable for any garden. Dark, green-grey leaves, 300mm/12in long and half as wide, sprout up in tufts from a semi-woody procumbent stem. The dark blue flowers, flecked white, grow in clusters on long, wiry stems, up to 1m/3ft high, and appear most of the year.

### Liriope muscari
H 350mm/14in  s 400mm/16in  −9°C/16°F  n f c 3
Liriope looks like a clump of dark, coarse grass, and bears upright spikes of purple flowers. It is similar to and easily confused with its relative, the pale lilac *Ophiopogon jaburan*. Both make good ground cover (soil cover for trees in containers) or plants to line a path.

### Nepeta × faassenii
H 600mm/24in  s 800mm/32in  −9°C/16°F  n a c 2
This catmint is a grey-green, semi-prostrate plant with lavender-blue flowers in spring and autumn. It is not unattractive and is resistant to poor conditions. Shear off dead flowers and cut back hard in early spring.

### Ophiopogon *see* Liriope muscari

### Osteospermum
This genus includes several perennial sub-shrubs and a perennial creeper that have produced a number of hybrids and cultivars ideal for the border or pots. They are allied to the annual dimorphothecas, and are often called by this name. They can be roughly divided into the ground covers, based on *O. fruticosum*, and the more shrubby types based on *O. jucundum* and *O. ecklonis*.

The members of this second group are truly perennial and an essential element in any garden. They can be reproduced by cuttings in summer or autumn and need very little watering.

Members of the first group are usually grown from seed sown in late winter and are best used as temporary fillers, as they seem to revert to plants with plain yellow flowers, by reseeding, after a few years. You can propagate them by cuttings, too, but not all are as successful as the famous 'Copper King'. They are not drought resistant and need watering every two weeks.

All gazanias are sun-lovers and the flowers only open in heat – most showily from spring to midsummer and intermittently thereafter. They do well in most soils, but prefer light, well-drained sites. All are hardy to −7°C/19°F.

### Lavandula dentata
H 1m/3ft  s 1.5m/5ft  −9°C/16°F  d a c i
This lavender species is the best for dry summer climates. It is more resistant than others to drought, has a longer blooming season and makes a bigger bulk; thus it is a useful plant for a dense, but shortlived hedge. The dark purple flowers have a rather different smell to *L. angustifolia*, the lavender from which the scented oil is distilled. The best variety of *L. angustifolia* is 'Grappenhall' which grows well, is dense and has very silver

*Osteospermum*

In the first group come plants with purple or blue-white flowers, both with very dark centres. They form wide mats of creeping stems that will reach 1.5m/5ft in diameter in a year while remaining only 200mm/8in high. The second group are at least twice as high but do not spread much more than 800mm/32in. Their flowers vary in colour from different shades of purple, through pink ('Pink Whirls'), to buff yellow ('Buttermilk'). One of the most striking, 'Tauranga', has white spatulate petals with a blue-purple reverse.

All flower in winter and early spring, sporadically at other times. They only need moderate watering, good soil, full sun and occasional cutting back to preserve a compact shape. Otherwise they are undemanding and trouble free.

## Pelargoniums

There are many species of these plants, popularly but incorrectly called geraniums, most with flowers which are not showy but some with attractive or strongly scented leaves. The rose-scented geranium *(P. graveolens)*, with deeply cut leaves, is one of the commonest and the apple-scented geranium *(P. odoratissimum)* and *P. tomentosum* are also commonly found, the latter being well suited to ground cover with its large, velvety leaves strongly scented of peppermint. The hybrids are divided into four main classes. The Uniques are generally old varieties of diverse parentage but include some of the most charming and characterful sorts, often with attractively marked flowers or scented foliage; 'Crimson Unique' and 'Madame Nonin'' are among the best. Zonal geraniums (*P.* × *hortorum*) are the ones most commonly seen, as pot plants, in bedding or in window boxes. They are available with flowers in almost any of the colours that lie towards the red end of the spectrum, plus purple and white, but excluding yellow. It is considered an asset if the leaves show a dark zone or horseshoe (except for those of white-flowered varieties which genetically cannot), and some varieties are cultivated solely for the colour variegations of the foliage.

Geraniums are easily grown from cuttings. Growing from seed gives stronger and denser garden plants but only for the single-flowered varieties that are more suitable for bedding. The select, often double, kinds do not come true from seed and are propagated from cuttings: these are better for pots and window boxes. Both are killed by temperatures below 0°C/32°F but in frost-free places they form woody bushes up to 1m/3ft high.

The major snag to what are otherwise excellent plants is their susceptibility to 'black leg', a fungal stem rot and several fungal rust diseases that pock the underside of the leaves with blackish or reddish spots. A fungicide may help but the only certain way to be rid of them is to grub up the plants and start again after a six-month interval.

The ivy-leaved geranium, *P. peltatum*, has more succulent, less hairy leaves than the zonal geranium and is a creeper-hanger-climber. It is nearly disease free and much to be recommended. The 'Balcon' series, derived from 'Roi des Balcons' and 'Ville de Paris', have narrow petals that do not overlap and smaller flowers but borne in such profusion that they are the showiest of this class.

The regal pelargonium, *P.* × *domesticum*, has a more shrubby form, larger, more crinkled leaves and beautiful and often multicoloured blossoms. It flowers only for a month in spring, though odd flowers may appear in autumn. The plant tends to look rather scraggy during the summer. Pinch back the growing tips but do not cut back far into old wood.

## Phormium tenax

H 2.5m/8ft s 1.5m/5ft −9°C/16°F n f c

The fibres obtained from its leaves gave rise to the common name of this leathery evergreen: the New Zealand flax. It makes an upright clump of swordlike leaves, springing from a common base. A popular variety is 'Veitchianum' with palish green leaves, striped yellow; it is a handsome plant that does not revert. The flower heads, not always seen, consist of clusters of red and yellow tubular blooms on zig-zag stems. It is very tough and will grow too big for many gardens, especially if well watered; smaller hybrids between this species and *P. cookianum*, with leaves of many colours (purple, bronze and red), are now being produced

### Polygonum capitatum
H 300mm/12in S 400mm/16in −2°C/28°F o f c
This is a neat, but tough and invasive ground cover, good for difficult places – it is one of the few plants that will grow under pine. Each plant multiplies rapidly and spreads by means of ground-hugging runners that have zoned leaves, marked pink in age, and small round heads of pink flowers during most of the year. Do not plant it in flower beds, but keep it for 'wild' areas or beds isolated by paving. Since it is only half-hardy, it will not survive deep or prolonged frost.

### Strelitzia reginae
H 1.2m/4ft S 1m/3ft −2°C/28°F n s c 1
The curious spiky yellow and orange crests of the bird of paradise flower are so arresting and unusual, and last so well in water, that they have become a highlight of flower shops throughout the world and the official flower of the city of Los Angeles. Strelitzia also makes an excellent plant for pots, or narrow beds on terraces, where the elegant foliage, like a short broad spear, is in itself decorative all year round. Being a member of the banana family it will only stand light frosts, and temperatures of −2°C/28°F may well damage the flowers and foliage. The rootstock may survive temperatures down to −4°C/25°F and sprout again. Many of the selected varieties are even less hardy, and are best grown as pot plants to be brought indoors during the winter. Strelitzia needs rich earth, frequent and heavy feeding, summer watering and good light. The flowers come during spring and autumn and again during the winter if not caught by frosts.

A much larger relative, *S. nicolai*, has leaves and stalks that may grow to more than 8m/26ft, eventually developing a palmlike trunk and bearing large, but not particularly eye-catching, white and bluish flowers. It is a superb foliage plant for larger frost-free gardens.

### Thymus
Thyme is an excellent choice for rockeries or paving cracks for it has tidy growth, fragrant flowers and foliage, and will survive being walked on, provided that

*Strelitzia reginae*

this does not happen too often. It is very pretty in flower for a month in the summer.

### Thymus vulgaris
H 350mm/14in S 1m/3ft −9°C/16°F d a c 3
The common thyme is the one most often used in cooking. It forms a rather open, wiry bush with small grey-green leaves and the heads of purple flowers produced in midsummer are loved by bees. The variegated *T. × citriodorus* 'Argenteus' makes denser growth.

### Vinca major
H 800mm/32in S 3m/10ft −9°C/16°F o f 2
The greater periwinkle will naturalize, but looks better and flowers more abundantly with occasional watering and feeding. The creeping, rooting stems make it rather invasive; it is better kept out of flower beds but it is at home under trees where not much else will grow. The blue flowers are not always a pure, clear colour.

### Viola odorata
H 100mm/4in S 200m/8in −9°C/16°F n a 1
The sweet violet makes an excellent ground cover in the shaded beds of a patio or along the shaded side of a wall. It is easy to grow, flowers from early spring to midsummer and spreads quickly by runners. *V. cornuta*, also with fragrant violet-coloured flowers, is similarly useful but is clump-forming.

# ANNUALS

The word 'annuals' conjures up images of sweeping lawns sectioned and ringed by banks of scarlet salvias and a wealth of golden marigolds. But these days few of us have the space to go in for traditional bedding on a large scale. What we may have is a small bed along the foot of a wall, a patch of earth in the middle of a patio, or some big pots that we want to fill with a colourful display. Most annuals have now been bred to flower steadily throughout their lives, and in a frost-free climate this may well exceed twelve months.

There are, of course, two ways of dealing with bedding plants. You can sow the seeds directly where you want them to flower, or you can buy the plants ready grown from a nursery. Growing from seed is cheap, but entails hard work in preparing a fine seed bed, in weeding during the time it takes for the plants to cover the ground, in thinning out seedlings and in watering them carefully without washing them out of the ground. It is much more expensive to buy plants, but as the plants you buy are probably in flower already, you will wait less time to see the results of your planning.

Plants that grow quickly or don't take happily to being transplanted are more suitable for direct seeding. This group includes eschscholzia, helianthus, marigolds, *Phlox drummondii*, sweet peas and zinnias. Unless you are a keen and expert gardener with time to spare, you will do best to buy plants of ageratum, antirrhinums, catharanthus, impatiens, pansies, petunias, primulas, salvias and verbena. Lobularia, calendulas and helichrysums can be treated either way.

The best bedding plants for full sun are probably pansies for winter and petunias for summer; in shade, cyclamen are good for winter and impatiens for summer. Marigolds are really something apart. Not everyone likes their colour or the smell of their foliage, but selective breeding is improving both, and they are spectacular plants that will flower profusely all year round, in sun or shade.

In the notes below, 'F1 hybrid' after the name indicates that you should plant only F1 plants, since these will be outstandingly better in most ways than open-pollinated varieties. As the majority of annuals will be killed by any frost, minimum temperatures have not been given. Plant out at two-thirds of the width figure.

---

### Ageratum (F1 hybrid)

H 150mm/6in  S 250mm/10in  m 3

This is a long-flowering plant, blooming throughout summer and autumn. It is usually found in various intense shades of blue – from deep purple to sky blue – but white and pink varieties are also available. They do best in a little shade and need watering. Try three in a large bowl surrounded by white alyssum, or a group planted as a border to a small bed of roses.

### Antirrhinum (F1 hybrid)

H 400mm/16in  S 300mm/12in  n 2

In Mallorca tall red antirrhinums are naturalized on banks and walls. These are, presumably, feral reseedings from garden plants and show that the snapdragon is a plant well adapted to hot, dry conditions. However, rust can be a problem, so buy rust-resistant varieties, which come in a range of vivid shades of red, pink, white and yellow. Most flower in late spring, but some modern varieties flower much earlier.

### Calendula officinalis

H 300mm/12in  S 300mm/12in  n c 1

This winter-flowering marigold cheers up the lowest moments of the year. The plants are either large, with brilliant orange or yellow blooms, or low-growing in mixed, slightly buff, yellows, creams and apricots, with darkish centres. All are very easy to grow.

### Catharanthus roseus

H 300mm/12in  S 300mm/12in  o c 3

Only in the warmest spots can this herbaceous member of the oleander family be grown successfully as a perennial. Elsewhere it will die in winter, or look so sorry that one does better to treat it as an annual – growing it, perhaps, as a terrace pot plant. Given enough heat, moderate sun or light shade, light watering and occasional feeding it displays periwinklelike flowers in pink, white or white with a red eye, over dark green glossy foliage; these flowers are produced over a long period. The Madagascar periwinkle grows easily from seed, but needs starting early indoors in a warm place.

### Celosia cristata

H 450mm/18in  S 450mm/18in  o 2

*Celosia cristata plumosa* has feathery plumes in red and yellow and *C. cristata* has distinctive 'cockscombs' both in red and yellow. They should be sown in early spring in their final flowering position, as they hate shocks and transplant badly.

*Impatiens walleriana* hybrid

### Eschscholzia californica
H 500mm/20in  s 250mm/10in  o 2
The California poppy is a beautiful silky-flowered Californian wild plant that needs no watering, and bears flowers in shades of bright red, orange and yellow.

### Helichrysum bracteatum
H 600mm/24in  s 500mm/20in  n 2
The strawflower is valuable both as a flowering plant for the garden and for the dried flowers that last almost indefinitely. One of the most flamboyant varieties is 'Bright Bikini', a dwarf mixture of pink, red, orange and yellow flowers.

### Impatiens (F1 hybrids)
Impatiens are popular bedding plants that are almost always used as annuals, though, planted in a warm frost-free corner, they will flower through the winter.
### Impatiens walleriana hybrids
H 300mm/12in  s 600mm/24in  m 2, 3
Commonly known as Busy Lizzie, the modern F1 hybrids make superb garden plants, flowering with abandon all summer. The colour range is wide and embraces reds and roses, while the 'star' varieties have white or pink flowers with red eyes. There are also double varieties which, although very pretty, are not so floriferous.

### Impatiens New Guinea hybrids
These plants are the result of intensive hybridizing between half a dozen new species found in Papua New Guinea. They vary in height and spread, but all have large lanceolate leaves which are of various colours, including bronze, green and green variegated with pink, yellow and cream. They have larger flowers than the Busy Lizzies but do not bear them with the same freedom. They are usually recommended for pots, but many of them make excellent bedding plants because they are even more resistant to the sun than their relative. In places without frost they are perennial.

### Lathyrus odoratus
H 2m/6ft  s 750mm/30in  o 2
Early sweet pea varieties can be sown from mid-autumn onwards, for precocious flowering. The bush kinds need no staking and reach a height of about 750mm/30in. Late sowing will not be satisfactory, as the heat of early summer will wither the seedlings.

### Linum grandiflorum 'Rubrum'
H 500mm/20in  s 150mm/6in  o 2
This crimson-flowered flax is an annual but it grows well and seeds itself so freely that you can think of it as a perennial that will return year after year. Sow the seeds in early autumn where it is to flower. 'Rubrum' looks especially good sown in drifts in wild gardens.

### Lobularia maritima
H 150mm/6in  s 400mm/16in  n 1, 2
Sweet alyssum is a very adaptable plant that forms mounds covered in fragrant flowers. The modern hybrids are dwarf, compact and come in a range of colours, including pure white, purple and rose. They will grow easily from seed, flowering within six weeks of germination and, with occasional watering, will continue to flower until the early frosts; in mild areas, alyssum is perennial, though shortlived.

### Petunia (F1 hybrids)
H 300mm/12in  s 450mm/18in  n c 2, 3
This most popular of summer bedding plants is easy to grow, happy in full sun and tolerant of a little dryness at the root. It is now produced in a wide range of plain, veined, starred, picotee, light-eyed and double flowers in almost every colour; great care is needed in choosing colours that do not clash. It suffers from chlorosis, especially if well watered, so be free with iron chelate and feed regularly. Pinch back the growing shoots after planting out, and whenever the plant becomes leggy,

From left to right: petunias, pansies and snapdragons

in order to encourage flowering. In frost-free areas petunias can be grown as winter-flowering annuals.

### Phlox drummondii

H 250mm/10in  S 250mm/10in  O 3

These colourful small annuals are used as bedding plants in India - proof that they will take heat and sun. Seedlings transplant badly and so are not normally supplied by nurseries, but phlox is easily grown from seed. Pinch back the growing tips and shear off dead heads to encourage continuous flowering.

### Primula (F1 hybrids) (Polyanthus and Primrose)

H 400mm/16in  S 300mm/12in  M 1

The polyanthus and the primrose behave very similarly when grown as annual bedding or pot plants. In theory the polyanthus has a bunch of flowers on a single stalk, the primrose a similar bunch but springing directly from the crown of the plant. However, in places where the winter temperatures rise above 20°C/68°F plants that behave as primroses in cold climates form flower scapes like the polyanthus. Modern hybridizing has helped to blur the distinction even further.

As bedding plants they both need to be put into the ground in early spring, or even late winter, and certainly before they begin flowering. They prefer moist beds at the foot of shaded walls and, though they will accept full sun, they will not grow as big or last as long. In theory both are perennials but the heat and low humidity of summer usually defeats them. However, though one thinks of primroses, particularly, as plants of shady woodland margins and wet meadow banks, if grown as annuals they do surprisingly well in hot climates.

### Salvia splendens

H 300mm/12in  S 750mm/30in  N C 3

Though this plant is best known in its brilliant scarlet form, there are also varieties in a mixture of purples, lavender and salmon. Modern varieties are much branched from the base and last far longer. You can sow from late winter until the early weeks of spring, but the small plants should not be planted out until all danger of frost has passed.

### Tagetes (F1 hybrids for T. erecta)

Marigolds are among the most frequently planted of summer bedding annuals. This popularity is justified, as they are cheap to grow from seed, easy and trouble free in cultivation, and flower the whole year round. They come in two kinds. Those based on *T. erecta*, the African marigold, have huge heads of double flowers on plants between 300mm/12in and 800mm/32in tall. The lower-growing types based on *T. patula*, the French marigold, are between 150mm/6in and

Marigolds

Pansies

450mm/18in tall, with smaller flowers, single or double, often marked russet and more freely produced. Sports and hybrids are blurring this distinction.

## Verbena
H 200mm/18in S 600mm/24in O 2, 3

Although shortlived perennials in frost-free areas, the garden verbenas are best treated as annuals, and are ideal for rather dry places – including rocky banks and dry-built terrace walls. They are good in pots and raised beds and come in two kinds – upright and spreading – both with very brightly coloured flower-heads in white or purples, usually with a white eye. They thrive in the sun, have a long flowering season and are drought resistant, though the garden varieties do better with occasional watering.

## Viola
Botanists include pansies, violas, and violets together in this genus. Although most are theoretically perennials, only the violets can be so treated. Even when grown in damp shade pansies and violas suffer too much from the heat and drought of summer to be worth keeping and so are best treated as annuals.

## Viola × wittrockiana (F1 hybrids)
H 200mm/8in S 350mm/14in m 1

The pansy is the mainstay bedding plant of the winter and spring. Pansies can be planted out before the plants show any blooms, from mid-autumn onwards. They like rich rather damp soil and light shade, though they do not mind direct sun until the intensity begins to build up from early spring.

The new F1 varieties are a great improvement in terms of quantity, duration and size of flower and are available in most colours, either plain faced, blotched with black, or with bicoloured and tricoloured faces. Shade prolongs the season at both ends and results in bigger plants and more flowers. Once spring gives way to the increasing heat of summer, the flowers become smaller and smaller until they are so insignificant that it is best to dig them up and plant new summer bedding plants.

## Zinnia
H 750mm/30in S 400mm/16in m 3

No other annual gives such a variety of effect, colour and size in such a short time. You can find dwarf varieties that grow 300mm/12in high and giants that grow 1.2m/4ft tall in a wide selection of flower shapes and colours. Zinnias grow rapidly from seed and need planting out before they bloom to make good specimens. The seed germinates in around five days and the plants flower within six to eight weeks. For continuous blooming, plant them in succession from the end of winter onwards until midsummer. F1 seed, whether of the dwarf or the tall varieties, is expensive, but you do not need many plants to make an effect and the germination rate is high. Zinnias like a weekly soaking, and plenty of food. Try to keep the foliage dry to avoid mildew, which will – in any case – catch hold of plants late on in the season, unless you are extremely lucky or spray them frequently.

# BULBS, CORMS, TUBERS AND RHIZOMES

Plants that develop from bulbs, corms, tubers or rhizomes are invaluable assets in the low-maintenance garden. These structures are designed to maintain plants in a resting state during periods unfavourable to growth, and to store reserves of food to help them get going again when good conditions return. As many plants of this type are indigenous to hot, dry regions, they rest – so require no water – during the summer drought, which is the period of adversity.

Although they need little attention, they should be given a good feed, preferably with a long-lasting organic mixture that is low in nitrogen, when the shoots first begin to show, and again when the leaves are at maximum development. This will enable the bulbs to replenish their reserves. If they are not well fed, most bulbs – narcissus, for example – will slowly become more and more impoverished, and finally fail to flower. Nourished and left alone so that the foliage dies down naturally they will grow and multiply.

Bulbs make excellent container flowers. Plant them densely for good effect, almost touching. As a rule of thumb, they should be planted at twice their own depth, that is, with the top of the bulb covered in its own depth of soil. After planting, in early or mid-autumn, leave the pots or bowls outside, preferably under moist sand. Remove the sand when the shoots begin to show, but do not bring bulbs into the house until the flower buds are well formed. Keep them watered until the foliage dies; most types can then be planted out in the garden, where they will take care of themselves.

Agapanthus

*Amaryllis belladonna*

## Agapanthus

H 1m/3ft  S 1m/3ft  −6°C/21°F  m f c 3

As well as being impressively ornamental, agapanthus is of enormous practical use, being tough and healthy, long-lived and undemanding. It is spectacular in flower and makes an excellent tub plant, while it is also one of the few flowers that will grow in the shade and among the roots of trees. To get the best results the bulbs need to be planted in rich earth mixed with peat or leaf-mould, in a lightly shaded situation. Ideally the soil should be watered well during the summer but kept quite dry during the winter. Agapanthus flowers best if it is potbound, or packed closely together in the open ground where the clumps of impressive erect stems will benefit from being divided every six to eight years.

The two evergreen species commonly grown are *A. africanus* and *A. praecox orientalis*. The first is relatively small, growing to 600mm/24in, while the second reaches 1.5m/5ft and is the more rewarding if you have the space. Both species are sometimes sold as *A. umbellatus*. There is also a white form *A. praecox orientalis* 'Albus' (rather hard to find as a bulb), a dwarf kind called 'Peter Pan' and semi-dwarf called 'Queen Anne' that is deciduous. All species grow well from seed but take three years to mature. (The cultivars will not breed true to type.) Divide clumps, or plant new bulbs in late summer or early autumn, cutting the leaves to half their length at the same time. Do not let the roots dry out at this stage. Transplanted bulbs may not flower during their first year.

## Amaryllis belladonna

H 500-800mm/20-32in  S 300-450mm/12-18in  −7°C/19°F  d f 4

This long-lasting bulb will naturalize well in hot, dry climates and bears a beautiful cluster of silvery pink, fragrant trumpet flowers at the top of the tall stalk in late summer, before the leaves appear. The bulbs should be kept dry during summer but you can anticipate the autumn rains by starting to water and feed a little before they come. Watering and feeding should both be increased as the leaves grow out after flowering. Plant with the neck of the bulb at ground level in a light, rich organic soil, and let them crowd for better flowers.

## Anemone coronaria

H 50-250mm/2-10in  S 100-150mm/4-6in  −7°C/19°F  d a c 1

Considering how colourful it is when flowering and the ease with which it grows, it is surprising that this spring-flowering perennial is not planted more often, especially the single De Caen strain and the semi-double, 'Saint Brigid'. *A. fulgens* is also eye-catching. The small bulbs should be planted 50mm/2in deep in mid-autumn, either in the open ground or in pots so that they can be brought into the house, if wished, when they begin to flower in early spring. They prefer a rich, moist earth lightened with some sand and peat. All need a sunny site and will probably seed themselves.

## Anemone × hybrida

H 1.5m/5ft  S 600mm/24in   −9°C/16°F  m a 3

White varieties such as 'Honorine Jobert' (syn. *A.* × *hybrida* 'Alba'), placed against a dark background, are among the most beautiful of garden plants. Japanese anemones need medium shade and must be kept moist-rooted all the summer to flower well in the autumn.

## Canna

H 1.5m/5ft  S 500mm/20in  −7°C/19°F  m f 3

If you want to give a corner an exotic feeling plant these showy perennials. The 1-2m/3-6ft stalks of large, often bronzy, leaves bear dishevelled heads of large petals in colours at the yellow to red end of the spectrum. A yellow variety almost twice this height is useful for obtaining quick effects. Grow the fleshy rhizomes in good moist soil.

## Clivia miniata hybrids

H 400mm/16in  S 300-600mm/18-24in  −3°C/27°F  m f 2

The Kaffir lily is a beautiful plant, with heavy, strap-shaped leaves and flower heads of orange trumpets in early spring. It accepts deep shade and likes a light, rich, well-draining leaf mould. Keep it as dry as possible during winter, but water all through the growing season. Like other amaryllis, clivias will not flower the first year after planting and will flower best if crowded.

## Crocosmia

H 1m/3ft  S 500mm/20in  −9°C/16°F  n a 3

The crocosmia has been growing in popularity, partly as a result of the large and showy new varieties such as 'Lucifer' and 'Dazzler' produced by the English nursery, Blooms of Bressingham. It looks best when it has made a clump of some size with its sword-shaped leaves. The long flower stalks bear a succession of yellow through orange to deep red flowers in late summer, and are best in some shade.

## Cyclamen

H 250mm/10in  S 350mm/14in  −5°C/23°F  d a 1

The cyclamen is a plant of character, distinction and quality, even though selective breeding in modern varieties has gone some way towards sacrificing these attributes in the search for greater flower size. All of the twenty or so species of cyclamen grow wild around the Mediterranean, so they should all prosper if planted in a dry garden. This is equally true of the large-flowered pot varieties, which are derived from *C. persicum*; (despite the species name, this is not a native of Persia but of the coasts of the northeastern Mediterranean).

The charm of the wild cyclamen is the demure but modestly proud carriage of its dainty downward-facing flowers with their upswept petals, growing over compact, densely tiered leaves. The breeders' efforts have concentrated too much, over the years, on huge flowers of stronger colours. In these varieties, one or more of the flower petals is nearly always frustrated by the stalk in its efforts to reflex itself. The leaves seem to be more irregular and are often prominently marked with lustrous silver; this may cause no conflict if the flowers are white but the silver looks less attractive when matched with pink or red flowers. In recent years miniatures, and varieties with fragrant flowers, seem to be making a comeback, though even with the miniatures some of the natural grace of the wild flower seems to have been lost.

The colours of different varieties compete, so it is advisable to stick rigidly to one colour. If you have a taste for variety, grade your planting from white at one end through pink to the reds at the other, trying to maintain the same type of leaf-markings throughout. This is easier said than done, as the plant is inherently

*Canna* 'President Kennedy'

variable. Even F1 varieties, though much more consistent, are still more variable than most first generation hybrids.

To grow cyclamen successfully in a pot you must give them the kind of conditions that you would find in light woodland in the Mediterranean in winter. They do not like being brought into a hot, dry room and will much prefer a light corner of the terrace or an outside windowsill where normal winter conditions prevail. Temperatures down to freezing will not harm them; the flowers, and the foliage of silver-leaved varieties, will suffer at −4°C/25°F, although the plants will not be killed off at this temperature.

All cyclamen, including the large-flowered florist's varieties, will grow perfectly well out of doors, under deciduous trees, in gaps in paving, at the bottom of open stone walls and even as massed bedding plants. Therefore, when your potted plant is beginning to look a bit yellow in late spring, gradually stop watering it and let the soil dry out completely. Plant the corm, which will probably be 60-90mm/2.5-3.5in across, somewhere in the garden and forget about it. In succeeding years (and particularly the first), it will probably not flower as generously as it did when you bought it, but the patterned leaves and succession of winter flowers will continue to charm you for the rest of your life – for, if the cyclamen is happy, it will outlive you.

## Cymbidiums and other orchids

Cymbidium hybrids seem to grow happily out of doors in shaded, frost-free places, preferably in a shade house where the humidity in summer can be maintained rather higher than in the open air. The plants most commonly available are spring-flowering miniature varieties, but though these are excellent for the house the large-flowered kinds are more spectacular for garden use.

Paphiopedilums with plain green leaves will also grow and flower in an unheated shaded greenhouse if not left to dry out, and a number of other genera can be grown in favoured spots. In the nineteenth century Mrs Hanbury was growing *Dendrobium anosmum* (syn. *D. superbum*), *Oncidium bifolium* and *Laelia anceps* in the open air on the branches of a large *Ficus indica* tree at La Mortola on the Riviera. The dendrobium gave the best effect: 'fairylike' she says.

As a rule orchids will only grow in shade that filters out at least 50 percent of the intensity of the sunlight. Water very little in winter but freely while the plant is putting on new growth in summer, feed lightly but frequently with general fertilizer and damp down daily, if you can, early in the morning. Use rainwater if possible, as orchids do not like hard water, which is high in calcium. Commercial growers usually pot cymbidiums in rock wool, but a very sharp-draining mixture that holds moisture – such as shredded bark mixed with peat and a little earth – is just as effective.

### Dahlia
H 2m/6ft s 2m/6ft 2°C/36°F o a 4
The dahlia, coming from Mexico and Guatemala, is an ideal garden plant if you have the means to water it, and the energy to dig up the tubers in the autumn and to prepare the ground thoroughly when you plant them out again in the spring. There are now several dwarf kinds that you can grow from seed. Most dahlias can be left in the ground over winter provided that the ground is not waterlogged and that the weeds are kept under control. Dahlias like a fairly rich soil, so give a light application of any fertilizer low in nitrogen in the spring, as they start into growth, and again as the flower buds show around midsummer.

### Dietes
This is a genus of tidy, long-flowering, irislike plants of some distinction that will look admirable in any garden. They need occasional watering, good soil and full sun.
### Dietes vegeta syn. Dietes iridioides
H 1.2m/4ft s 1m/3ft −5°C/23°F d a 3
This evergreen perennial forms a substantial clump of stiff, swordlike leaves. For much of the year it bears white flowers with orange centres.

Cymbidium orchids

### Freesia
H 250mm/12in s 100mm/4in −5°C/23°F d a 2
Gone are the days when freesias used to bear beautifully formed, small, creamy flowers with an exquisite fragrance. They have now become large, sometimes double, rather blowzy flowers in a wide range of not very attractive colours, and they have nearly lost the delightful smell that was once their greatest asset. The old semi-wild variety self-seeded with abandon. The new sorts seem less prodigal. All like rich, gritty, open soil, moist during the winter, but, as the foliage yellows after flowering, almost drying out for the summer.

### Hemerocallis
H 1m/3ft s 750mm/30in −9°C/16°F n a c 3
For a plant that used to be recommended solely for damp, waterside locations, the modern hybrid day lily is extraordinarily undemanding. It still likes watering, especially when flowering, but will survive with little if necessary. The lilylike flowers (that individually last a day) are now found in many shades and bicolours of yellow, buff, pink, red, rust and maroon, some double. Best planted where they will receive sunlight for part of the day, they are disease free and their large grassy clumps of foliage suppress weeds. They flower for a month between late spring and early autumn, according to the variety, some for two shifts.

*Ipheion uniflorum*

## Ipheion uniflorum

H 150mm/6in  s 50mm/2in  −9°C/16°F  d a 2

These pretty bulbs, also sold as *Milla, Brodiaea* and *Triteleia*, bear small, pale blue, star-shaped flowers with flat faces in later winter, and naturalize easily in grass. 'Froyle Mill' is a rich mid-blue-violet and 'Rolf Fiedler' is a clear blue.

## Iris

Irises are broadly divided into those that grow from rhizomes and those that grow from bulbs. One of the most fundamental principles to observe when growing most members of this beautiful and diverse genus is to let the bulb or rhizome dry up and remain dormant. Watering during this period is prejudicial to many and even fatal to some.

The rhizomes should be planted to lie on the surface of the soil. The most popular members of this group are the tall bearded irises for which modern breeding has produced large, spectacular flowers in almost every colour and combination of colours. Hot, dry summers suit them and they are easy to grow. Some varieties may reach 1m/3ft in height. Their leaves and flowering stalks can be cut back to the ground after flowering. A major drawback, apart from a rather short season of bloom, is that the beds can quickly become infested with weeds – including Bermuda grass, which has a

habit of creeping among the iris beds from the lawn. Every few years you must dig up the rhizomes in the autumn and clean the beds before replacing them.

Of the rhizomatous types you may like to try some of the following.

## Iris unguicularis

H 600mm/24in  s 400mm/16in  −4°C/25°F  n a 2

The winter iris (syn. *I. stylosa*) from Algeria is an excellent, accommodating, tough plant that grows in dense clumps that smother weeds. It positively likes heat and drought during the summer and near-rubble rather than earth to grow in; it is excellent for narrow beds around house walls. The mid-blue (in some forms purple or white) flowers that appear among the narrow foliage in midwinter will stand out better if the leaves are sheared to half their length in early autumn, before the flower buds appear. Divide the clumps every few years at the same time of year. For flower arrangements, pull the flower stems from the plant, do not break or cut them.

## Iris japonica

H 350mm/14in  s 100mm/4in  −9°C/16°F  d a 1

This pretty little iris has rather orchidlike flowers in white, marked pale blue and gold. They are carried on branching stems in spring, and need good, moist soil and a little shade. 'Ledger's Variety' is an improved form.

## Oncocylus and Regelia irises

These and their hybrid progeny are all exquisitely beautiful irises with huge flowers in grey, pale blue, pale maroon and silver, all networked and reticulated in darker shades. But they are also extremely difficult to grow, especially oncocylus, the most beautiful. Put them in a mixture of rubble and rich earth on the top of a slightly shaded dry terrace wall and never water them – a challenge for enthusiasts with money, for the rhizomes are expensive.

The bulbous irises are not so numerous. Most need planting 100mm/4in deep.

## Iris reticulata

H 180mm/7.5in  s 70mm/3in  −9°C/16°F  d f 1

This miniature iris, with its fragrant blue flowers, is not very easy to grow, except in places with a number of frosts a year, but it is attractive in rockeries.

## Iris xiphium hybrids

H 600mm/24in  s 200mm/8in  −9°C/16°F  a 2

The Spanish and Dutch irises are beautiful tall spring-flowering plants in a range of many colours, all excellent as cut flowers. Give full sun and regular watering when growing, but let them dry off during the summer.

*Zantedeschia aethiopica*

## Narcissus

The many narcissus varieties will all naturalize well. Plant them deep down in mid-autumn, with the bottom of the bulbs 250mm/10in below the soil surface. A good site is beneath deciduous trees, since the bulbs like sun when growing and flowering, and shade for the rest of the year. Spread a general fertilizer, supplemented by some bonemeal, over the area where you know that the bulbs are buried some weeks before they are due to appear. Be careful not to give too much, or the new shoots underground will be burned.

## Ranunculus asiaticus

H 250mm/10in S 130mm/5in −3°C/27°F d a 2
With the arrival of Japanese extra-double, low-growing strains, the ranunculus has become an even more popular pot plant. It should be used more often outdoors in beds as a colourful carpet, for it returns reliably year after year. Consider planting a small bed with just one colour; the greeny white or the very pale pink, for example. In fact almost all the colours are of attractive tones, though some are very strong.

Plant the small 'claws' in mid-autumn, and put out pot-grown plants any time up to flowering, which begins in late spring.

## Sternbergia lutea

H 300mm/12in S 150mm/6in −9°C/16°F d a 4
This has a flower like a large yellow autumn crocus. It will naturalize readily and does well on chalk. Plant 150mm/6in deep but do not expect flowers the first year. Plant and divide in mid-autumn.

## Tulipa

The large-flowered hybrid tulips are best grown as annual pot plants but many species of tulips will naturalize readily. *T. clusiana* is one of the best, a dainty, small plant with cream petals striped pink. You might also try *T. praecox*, with its bright scarlet flowers and yellow base. *T. fosteriana* (scarlet), *T. kaufmanniana* (cream to yellow flushed pink), *T. saxatilis* (lilac with a yellow centre) and *T. sylvestris* (bright yellow within, greenish yellow without) are all worth growing. They should all be planted at a depth equal to at least three times the diameter of the bulb, and they need an annual top-dressing of a low-nitrogen fertilizer, following exactly the same regime as the naturalized narcissi.

## Zantedeschia aethiopica

H 1m/3ft S 500mm/20in −8°C/17°F m f c 2
The arum or calla lily will endure most conditions except for the extremes of sun or drought, but it relishes very damp, rich soil and half shade. It has ornamental leaves and beautiful white or cream hoods (or spathes), surrounding the small inner flowers. There are several other species and hybrids with yellow, green, pink and red hoods that are harder to grow and no more beautiful. All will look attractive whether grown in the open ground or in large containers. Plant the rhizomes at a depth of 150mm/6in about 450mm/18in apart.

## Zephyranthes grandiflora

H 200mm/8in S 200mm/8in −8°C/17°F d a 3
The zephyr or rain lily is a delightful member of any garden, and, as its common name suggests, it flowers after rain, putting out a pretty display of large, star-shaped flowers, like open crocuses, each having six to eight pink petals with rounded points. If you water deeply every fortnight, but then let the soil almost dry out in between, you will have flowers a couple of days later and you can go on repeating this pattern throughout the late summer and autumn. In winter they should be given little or no water and, if grown out of doors, may need covering to keep off excess rain. In colder areas they should be grown in a pot and brought indoors for the winter. Plant them 80-100mm/3-4in deep, preferably in a sunny, sheltered spot.

# CACTI AND SUCCULENTS

In regions that experience a long summer drought, cacti and succulents make excellent garden plants. They thrive in full sun, and effective drainage will ensure that they do not suffer too much from damp in winter. The deserts in which they grow are often cold at night, and most cacti and succulents will not mind a few degrees of frost. Indeed, to flower well many cacti actually need a certain degree of cold.

A steep, rocky hillside facing south, a position where both water and cold air will quickly drain away, makes the ideal site. The best that most gardeners can provide is a spot that gets full sun all day. It should preferably be protected by a wall, but free from the shade of trees or buildings. There should always be a wide path next to a cactus bed, especially if it is on a sloping site – the experience of falling full length into a bed of cacti is definitely one to be avoided.

Although cacti must be kept as dry as possible in winter, they all need an occasional watering in summer.

Succulents will also benefit from a thorough soaking from time to time. Both cacti and succulents need feeding during the spring and summer growing season.

Some cacti grow very fast, making a thicket as big as a tree or a clump the size of a small room. Others will never grow any larger than a golfball. As transplanting large cacti can be a painful process, it is important with these plants to make a careful initial planting plan, taking ultimate height and spread into account.

Some bear exquisite flowers. They usually last no more than a day or two, but this only adds to the poignancy of their beauty. There is something ineffably romantic in the way so delicate a flower is borne by such a fierce-looking object. Both of the two main types of succulent – the ground-covering, daisy-flowered plants that are usually classed together as mesembryanthemums or 'mesems', and the spiky-looking plants of the aloe and agave genera – bear flowers, some of them more or less continuously.

A crested cereoid cactus that resembles a piece of living sculpture

Cereus in flower

The hooked spines all the way down the leaf edges are even harder to deal with. If you want the plant to be tidy, cut off the bottom leaves close to the trunk when they begin to die.

After flowering, new plants will sprout up all over the place and the resulting jungle of spines is hard to remove. All things considered, big examples of both species are most impressive but definitely for the wilder areas of the garden or else kept under rigid control. Some of the other species, such as *A. victoriae-reginae*, are more manageable and less aggressive. Most can be moved, even when large, and can stand any drought.

Furcraeas are commonly grown in Mediterranean gardens but look so like agaves they are often mistaken for them. They will make a rosette of leaves 1-2m/3-6ft long and are most handsome in variegated forms such as *F. foetida* 'Striata' or *F. selloa* 'Marginata'.

Also agavelike is *Beschorneria yuccoides* from Mexico; it has bright coral-red flower stems up to 2m/6ft high with coral bracts and nodding green flowers.

### Aeonium canariense
H 1.5m/5ft  S 1.5m/5ft  −3°C/27°F  o a c 1
This fine large plant bears a large bushy head of small yellow flowers. The purple rosettes and miniature tree form of *A. arboreum* 'Atropurpureum' can look well in a pot. Both tend to become leggy, particularly if they are not watered from time to time.

### Agave
The agaves form huge rosettes of long, menacing spiked leaves. After about twelve years or so they throw up a vast flowering spike like a gigantic asparagus spear; this opens into a 'candelabrum' of yellow flowers at the top, after which impressive feat it dies. You will, however, often find that baby plants formed on the tops of the spike have scattered everywhere.

*Agave americana*, its variegated forms, and *A. sisalana*, which has narrower leaves and is the source of sisal, all have ornamental sword-shaped leaves, but are apt to cause trouble. They take up a lot of space – a mature plant can measure 4m/13ft across – and even if a plant is removed the roots left behind may propagate rampantly. The horrific spikes at the ends of the leaves are extremely dangerous, particularly since for many people they are at eye level. Clip off the ends of these spikes with secateurs, taking care not to cut into the leaf, which would then tend to shred and look untidy.

### Aloe
The members of this voluminous genus of spiky-fingered succulents usually flower during winter, when they bear tall torches of bright orange-red that light up the garden. They will grow in any gravelly soil or rubble and will flourish in the hottest, sunniest place you can find for them. Aloes flower best with an occasional watering during the summer, but they will do without. In time, a group will form a dense interlocking mass that keeps down all weeds. Some magnificent hybrids have been produced in California.

### Aloe arborescens
H 4m/13ft  S 4m/13ft  −2°C/28°F  d a c 3
Tall heads of scarlet flowers sprout early in the year from this aloe's dense mass of long, thick, spiky, curved leaves. Although temperatures of −2°C/28°F will cause damage, the plant will not be killed even by much greater cold. In frost-free places it may become very large, reaching 4m/13ft high and as much across.

*Aloe striata* is much smaller, with interlocking rosettes 450mm/18in across and heads of pink or red bell flowers on stalks even longer than this. Smaller still, *A. variegata* has green leaves, banded white in a triangular rosette only 200mm/8in across. It is good for pots or a rockery.

### Aptenia cordifolia
H 150mm/6in  S 600mm/24in  −1°C/30°F  o f
This relative of the mesembryanthemums makes an excellent ground cover in sun or light shade and needs

little watering, though it will take hardly any frost. The flowers are more or less continuous, if unspectacular, consisting of tiny red tufts sparsely distributed throughout the carpet of 25mm/1in leaves. Two selected varieties are also available: one with bright red flowers and strong growth, the other with purple flowers and smaller leaves.

## Cephalocereus senilis
H 2m/6ft  S 200mm/8in  −2°C/28°F  d f
The old man cactus is a columnar plant covered in long grey hair. It grows slowly to a great age; in its native Mexico ancient specimens are known of 10m/33ft or more. Plants of 2m/6ft high are rare and may be forty or fifty years old, but even small ones are distinctive and will be much remarked upon in any cactus garden.

## Cereus
This genus of columnar cactuses have spiny stems with pronounced ribs. They need well-drained soil and full sun, and are capable of withstanding temperatures down to −7°C/19°F.

## Echinocactus grusonii
H 1m/3ft  S 1m/3ft  −4°C/25°F  o f 2
This rather slow-growing, green, slightly flattened sphere, covered in sharp yellow spines, is known as 'Mother-in-law's cushion'. It looks best in groups and is tough, tidy and easily grown.

## Mesembryanthemum
Nurseries tend to group a large number of plants indiscriminately into the 'mesem' category, regardless of their botanical taxonomy. These can include members of the genera *Lampranthus, Drosanthemum, Malephora* and at least half a dozen more. All have small, daisy-shaped flowers often in very brilliant and startling colours, including various shades of purple, red, orange and yellow.

The different species that are likely to be found in nurseries are very seldom named, so you will have to make up your mind which you want when you see them. One genus that is fairly distinct is *Carpobrotus*, for it is on a much larger scale than the usual 'mesems', with leaves more than 50mm/2in long and three-sided. The South African species *C. edulis*, known as the Hottentot fig, has leaves 100mm/4in long and a yellow flower. The western North American species *C. chilensis* has purple flowers and smaller leaves that are straight rather than curved. Both are useful, especially on the coast.

*Opuntia ficus-indica* (background) and *Yucca aloifolia*

## Opuntia ficus-indica
H 4m/13ft  S 4m/13ft  −5°C/23°F  d f 2
The prickly pear is a large, gross cactus with leaves like green dishes attached to the arms. It grows quickly to 4m/13ft high and as wide. It was once widely cultivated for the orange-red, goose-egg-sized fruits (the prickly pears). These are ornamental – edible but not delicious – and, like the whole plant, are covered in irritating hairs. Any bit of the plant that falls to the ground develops roots and grows so fast that the prickly pear has become a weed in some hot countries, barely controlled by the caterpillar that feeds on it. The new growths are flat green and oval, the older ones more cylindrical and brown, so that kept in hand (and it must be a gloved hand unless you grow the cultivar 'Burbank's Spineless'), it can be quite decorative for really dry spots.

## Portulacaria afra
H 2m/6ft  S 3m/10ft  −4°C/25°F  d f
This resembles a miniature jade plant (*Crassula argentea*) with the same bonsai look and small, succulent bright green leaves on stout brown branches. It will take any amount of heat and sun and is drought proof and fire resistant. It is called elephant food in its native South Africa. In frost-free places it will grow to 2m/6ft in the open ground; though it makes a good container-grown specimen, it will then be much smaller.

# THE THREE FUNDAMENTALS

Before you can even begin to make a garden in any area with a Mediterranean climate, you will have to tackle the basic problem of how you are going to create favourable conditions for your plants. This is largely a matter of providing sufficient water, adequate soil, and, in many cases, a degree of shade.

If summers are hot and dry the amount of water available during those crucial months determines the character of the garden. It is quite possible to create a garden using only drought-resistant native plants. If, however, your aim is a garden of green lawns and bright flowers, you will have to provide a supply of pure water and a means of applying it. This can be a costly business: the water may well have to be brought by truck, and you may need to lay down an extensive network of pipes to distribute it around the garden. Improving the soil may similarly involve importing truckloads of good earth or organic supplements.

The provision of shade will, among other benefits, lower the temperature and reduce plants' need for water. Hedges, walls and trees all provide some shade; and by building a shade house, the more ambitious gardener can create suitable conditions for plants that require a higher degree of shade and humidity.

# WATERING

The worst aspects of the Mediterranean climate for plants are precisely those that make it so delightful for holidays – the hot sun and the almost total lack of rain during the summer months. The excess of evaporation over rainfall means that humidity falls, the countryside dries up, and all plants that are not adapted to these conditions die in the dry heat.

The native trees and shrubs have their own means of protection against these conditions. Some – such as the carobs, the lentisk, the olive and the holm oak – have foliage that is tough and hard, and therefore retains some moisture. Others – including cistus, rosemary and the almonds – desiccate, look dead and cease many of their functions until the rains return. But, without watering, the great majority of ornamental plants will find conditions too arid for survival. It is no exaggeration to say that the amount of water you are able, or prepared, to allocate to your garden fixes its type. If you have insufficient supplies, and find that the expense of water brought by lorry is too great, you will have to content yourself with a garden composed of plants that normally need no watering. This will restrict the number of species you can use, but you will gain by having a trouble-free garden that can be left unattended for eleven months of the year, which, for owners of holiday homes, is a great advantage.

## HOW MUCH, HOW OFTEN
Commercial growers consider that full irrigation in a Mediterranean climate, in high summer, requires the distribution of at least 50,000 litres per hectare per day (about 4,400 gallons per acre). On this basis, if your garden is 500 square metres/1,800 square feet, you need to apply 2,500 litres/550 gallons – the equivalent of twenty bathfuls of water or five hours with a hose – every day! Fortunately, there are a great many garden plants that do not need full irrigation, but, even so, in any garden that is not composed entirely of drought-resistant plants, watering by hand is likely to demand not only a great deal of time but also, in some cases, a lot of energy.

In the open ground, how often and how generously you need to water will depend on a variety of factors, including the individual needs of each species of plant (obviously, a tree is going to need a lot more water than a shallow-rooted annual), whether the site is exposed to full sun, whether the soil is heavy or light, and, of course, the weather. However, there is one important general principle: give twice as much water half as often. If you water lightly and frequently, the plant roots develop near the surface of the soil, where they are at risk should you be unable to water for a short time. If you make certain that the soil is well wetted down to a good depth, the roots will tend to grow downwards, seeking water as the surface dries out, and so will be less liable to dry out themselves. Needs vary so much that it is impossible to give more than a rough guide, but generally I would recommend watering every ten days at the rate of up to 40 litres per square metre/8 gallons per square yard. If soil is really dry, even this apparently large quantity of water will only wet it to a depth of 200mm/8in or so.

Container-grown plants need much more frequent watering. At the height of summer, the earth in a small black plastic pot can dry out in less than three hours, and the internal temperature will quickly rise to lethal heights. Clay pots are rather better, since they do not absorb so much heat and the evaporation of moisture through the porous clay walls has a cooling effect. However, all small pots standing in the sun need to be watered at least every day; watering every other day may be enough for larger containers and window boxes. All containers should be copiously watered, until a little liquid runs out of the bottom of the pot; this thorough irrigation has the beneficial effect of dissolving and flushing out any salts which, in concentration, would inhibit plant growth.

## WHEN TO WATER
Watering in the early morning helps the plant most, because it ensures that this factor, among all those critical to healthy development – warmth, light, food and water – is at a good level as the day's growth starts. However, it is common practice in Mediterranean countries to water in the evening, which is almost as effective since there is relatively little moisture loss from the soil at night. Except in an emergency, watering in the middle of the day is best avoided, especially in summer. The thermal shock of cold water on hot plants when active can be harmful, and drops of water may concentrate the sunlight, as through a lens, sufficiently to burn the foliage.

## WATERING LAWNS

The quantity of water required to keep a lawn green will vary depending on the type of grass. In very general terms, in full summer most lawns need 30mm/1¼in of water once in ten days, or 20mm/¾in every five days. This quantity of water is about the amount provided by the average sprinkler left to run for a couple of hours in one spot. You should never water a lawn more frequently than twice a week as this encourages surface rooting, with the result that, if you stop watering so frequently, the grass will suffer. Remember that no sprinkler applies an even watering over the whole area of its throw.

## WATERING OF BULBS AND RHIZOMES

The watering of bulbs and rhizomatous plants needs to be considered separately. The reason that a plant has developed these structures is to tide it over a difficult period, in the same way that a dormouse may hibernate when food is scarce. For wild bulbous plants, in most parts of the world, summer is the period of adversity, because of the drought. A wild narcissus, tulip or scilla grows fast during the relatively wet winter, but as the summer drought sets in the foliage dies; a storage organ is left in the dry ground, ready to burst into life again once the rains begin in the autumn.

Most of these plants flower early in the year, as soon as pollinating insects are flying in any numbers. The majority of bulbs start to produce their first foliage before the flowering spike develops, though there are a few plants, such as amaryllis and belladonna, that finish the flowering stage before they start to put on any leaves at all. All use their foliage to replenish the exhausted bulb, by photosynthesis, during the favourable growing conditions of the spring; they then dry up and return to the resting condition as the drought of full summer takes over.

This natural cycle provides the key to successful bulb cultivation indoors or in pots; outdoors they will look after themselves. In general, bulbs should be planted when the rains start. It is important to keep them cool, as well as watered, until the spring. Then you can expose them to the warmth as you simultaneously begin to restrict their water supply. From the beginning of summer, once the foliage begins to die back, you should keep them almost completely dry; begin to water them again in early autumn. The conditions in centrally heated houses are too warm in winter for many of these bulbs. Cyclamen, for instance, will grow better and last far longer as patio plants than indoors. Their foliage stays dense, low and hard, and they will continue flowering for three months or more.

The main group that needs treating differently includes all South African bulbs except those of the Western Cape. In the Transvaal and Natal winter is dry and cold and the rains come during the hot summer. Plants from these regions find it hard to adapt to winter rains and dry summers and grow best if you can water them well all summer and allow them to dry out in the winter. Even within this group there are some bulbs that are more adaptable than others. Agapanthus, for example, can be planted out in large masses under trees, where they get no water during the summer, and yet look healthy and flower well every year. But in general there is little doubt that you cannot give any of these bulbs, including agapanthus, too much water in the summer months or too little in winter.

## WATERING BY HAND

Water is a more complex subject than one might think. An army of gardeners with watering cans is best, from the plant's point of view, because you can give each one exactly the amount it requires. Even with a hose, very few people have the time, or patience, to give the garden the quantity of water it needs in the middle of summer. The simpler the task is made for the gardener, the more likely it is to be done. For this reason I strongly advocate the use of any system that makes the job easier, even if it consists of nothing more complicated than a series of taps, to which hoses can be attached, at strategic points around the garden.

For a small garden or terrace of drought-resistant plants that will need no more than a fortnightly soaking, irrigation by hose is quite practical, if tedious, and snap-lock fittings make this simple job even easier. They enable you to use short lengths of hose, link hoses together, join them to taps, or fit accessories; although most of these fittings are not, in my opinion, as robust as they should be, they are obviously extremely useful.

Long hoses are much harder to manage and are liable to damage bedding plants or even containers if pulled across the garden. You can make using a long hose a less risky business if you get the local ironmonger to cut some 300mm/12in lengths of reinforcement rods as thick as your little finger, and bend the top 100mm/4in of each through 45 degrees. Push or hammer these rods into the corners of your beds, with the curve facing away from the bed. As you pull your hose around the garden you can thread it round the hooks, and they will keep the hose in place and stop it whiplashing across your plants. You can sometimes find these hooks ready-made, with either small plastic balls

A hose has a will of its own; it kinks and blocks or blows off the tap fitting; it writhes and, if you drop it, water gouges holes in the soil; its coils are heavy and drag across your plants.

Hooks on the corners of beds and along the paths will help to keep lively hoses in place. Beads (*centre*) or rolling tubes (*right*) threaded on to the hooked rods ease friction as you pull the hose around the garden.

or rolling tubes threaded on to the curves, to ease the friction on the hose as it runs around them.

Many professional gardeners disdain to use a rose on the end of the hose, preferring to rely on their ability to place a thumb over the end to control the flow and produce anything between a jet and a fine rain. For most of us, however, a well-made rose has many advantages. In particular, it usually gives a far finer spray. If you do not want to use a rose, you will find that a useful accessory when watering a bed or a large pot is a coarse, heavy rag tied over the end of the hose. This ensures that the water oozes out of the material without disturbing the earth; an uncontrolled jet can gouge holes.

I always water newly planted material by hand, rather than relying on a sprinkler system. Until the roots of the cuttings or seedlings have developed extensively and deeply, they will need heavier and more frequent watering than normal. Consider carefully, too, the conditions under which the plant you are setting out was growing before you acquired it. Most nurseries nowadays have automatic watering and fertilizing systems and many grow some of their stock under shade. These three factors will induce a softish growth that is more likely to suffer when put out into drier earth and full sun. If you think that you will be giving your purchase a harder life than it was used to in the nursery, be attentive with the watering, particularly in the early days, and provide some shade. Lay palm fronds, branches of

evergreens, shade cloth or old net curtain over or around the plant: anything, in fact, that will cast some shade and give a little protection from drying winds. As soon as the plant begins to make new growth you can gradually remove the shade, but it is best to continue with a higher than usual level of watering during the first year.

## AUTOMATIC WATERING SYSTEMS

Automatic watering is a highly developed art these days and it is best to seek professional advice before installing an expensive system. It does help, though, to understand the basic options. Broadly speaking, there are two types of automatic watering systems: high-level and low-level.

High-level systems are based on pumps that pressurize the water and create 'rain' by means of a variety of spray-generating nozzles held well above the ground. These nozzles, which are small in number since each covers a wide area, are supplied with water, under the pressure of a few atmospheres, by pipes that are usually buried in the ground.

High-level watering systems are simple, robust and particularly useful for large areas. Because they distribute water in such a general, undirected way, however, they can be very wasteful, especially in a garden where quantities of water may fall on paths or terraces. There is also the problem that the spray may not reach the water-shadow on the far side of a large bush or tree. For this reason very careful placing of the nozzles is necessary. This method also tends to encourage the growth of weeds. As the whole surface of the ground is well watered, any weed seeds that are already lying there or that are blown on to the beds will germinate and multiply.

Low-level devices may produce drips or trickles – either under or on the soil surface – or a low-level spray

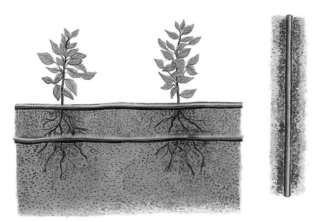

Permanent watering tubes can lie on the soil or be buried a palm's breadth below the surface to produce a deep but narrow 'line' of irrigation. You can use a porous 'seep hose' that leaks along its length or polythene tubing fitted with periodic emitters.

Drip emitters provide a steady dribble of water, wetting a column of earth about twice as deep as wide. Around a tree, you will need to space several emitters, on the end of microtubes, just within the farthest reach of the branches.

just above ground level. Until power pumps came into use a form of low-level watering was the only method available: nearly all watering was achieved by ploughing an earth channel with a hoe so as to divert water along the bed. Today most low-level irrigation systems are based on plastic tubing pierced by 'emitters' that allow the water to drip out at regular intervals. The pipes can be run around the garden so as to disperse water exactly where it is wanted.

On the whole, low-level watering is more economical of water, less encouraging to weeds, and probably better for plants than overhead systems. However, complicated networks of pipes and fine tubes lying on the surface are very easily disturbed: you can damage or dislodge them as you are weeding, and dogs and cats can uproot them. It is also much more difficult to be sure that water is issuing successfully from the tubes, because they easily become hidden by vegetation, than it is to see that overhead sprinklers are doing their job.

Most low-level systems work by producing a steady dribble of water which, if left on for an hour or more, will thoroughly wet the soil area immediately around the jet. You must be careful about the precise distribution of the emitters in order to avoid two disadvantages inherent in the system. The first is that the drip wets the soil to a greater depth – perhaps up to 1.2m/4ft below the surface – than width – 600-900mm/24-36in is typical. Therefore, most trees would need several emitters around their root zones. This zone rings the tree to a distance equivalent to the farthest reach of its branches, and the feeding roots

permeate the top 600mm/24in of the soil. Some species, especially those resistant to drought, have tap roots that go very much deeper; for these one emitter placed close to the trunk and left on infrequently, but for several hours at a time, provides the best method of watering. It enables you to economize on water by concentrating it on the tap root, which is the tree's primary means of taking up moisture.

The second disadvantage is that pressure differences in the tube, caused by variation in levels, produce disparities in the amount of water supplied along its length. If your garden is not flat you should fit special emitters, of which there are several different types, designed to emit a constant supply of water even when considerably different water pressures exist in different levels of the tubes.

Two problems are common to high- and low-level watering systems, but generally cause more difficulty with underfoot systems, as the outlets tend to be smaller. These are algal growths, which quickly colonize and block fine holes, and, in regions with hard water, deposits of calcium carbonate that form inside the tubes and, again, block the holes. You can cure the algae problem by passing dilute algicide through the tubes occasionally. Burying the tubes of a low-level system helps reduce water evaporation and, consequently, the level of calcium deposition, but if you have hard water you will still probably need to detach the nozzles and emitters occasionally and soak them in a mildly acidic solution, such as that sold for descaling kettles or a 10 per cent solution of hydrochloric acid.

## Irrigation control devices

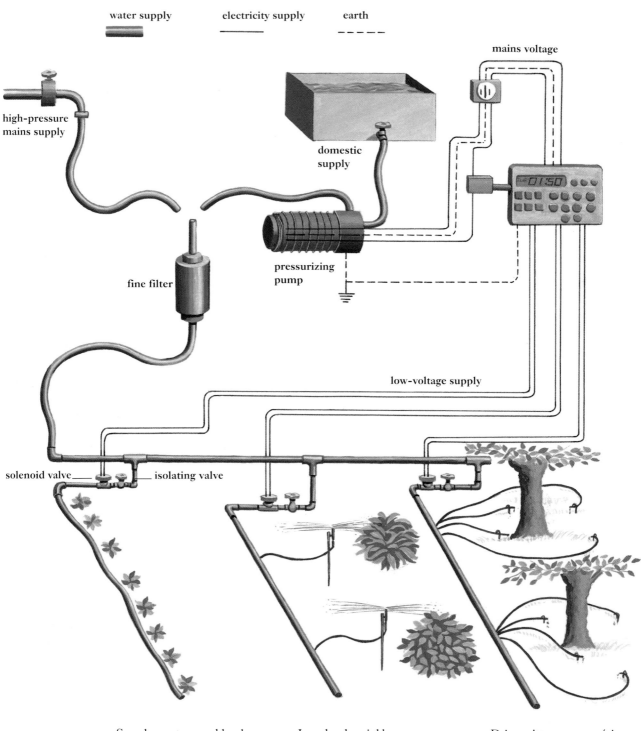

water supply

electricity supply

earth

mains voltage

high-pressure
mains supply

domestic
supply

fine filter

pressurizing
pump

low-voltage supply

solenoid valve          isolating valve

Seep hose at ground level

Low-level sprinklers,
50-300mm/2-12in high

Drip emitters, 100mm/4in
above ground

## CONTROL DEVICES

In order to manage the more sophisticated types of automatic watering systems, you need an adjustable timer/controller linked to a series of electric solenoid-operated water valves. Depending on the size of the garden and the fatness of your wallet, the controller can serve from one to a dozen or more valves. You can set the valves to open in sequence at any time of the day or night, for periods of perhaps a minute to an hour, any day of the week, up to several times a day. Most control devices have a connection for turning a pump on at the same time as they open any valve, and this is essential if you draw your water from a tank or a well, or if the mains water lacks sufficient pressure.

The output from these controllers, to the valves and the pump, is normally of much lower voltage than the mains supply. This is an important safety feature since a combination of water and high-voltage electricity can be highly dangerous. For the same reason it is essential to position the controller, which is fed by mains electricity, in a dry place. The automatic switch for your pump needs to have a solenoid whose voltage matches the output from the controller, and the whole system must be put together by a competent electrician.

All this sounds rather daunting, perhaps, but in practice such a system is cheaper and easier to manage than the pumps and filters of a swimming pool – and some people seem to get more pleasure out of tinkering with those than they do from swimming in the pool! The hardest part is deciding on the size of the tubes and valves. On the one hand, you want to avoid the expense of buying a system larger than your garden needs, and on the other hand, you need to be sure that the pipes are wide enough to carry water at the pressure required to work effectively.

Most manufacturers provide tables of pressure loss through pipes, and all the makers of micro-sprinklers will tell you how much each one delivers for a variety of pressures. With this information you should be able to work out what diameters you need. As a general guide, you will probably find that 25mm/1in tube is suitable for loops 30m/100ft long, two or three of which can branch off a supply tube of 30mm/1¼in diameter fed through a valve. As only one valve will be open at a time, the tube that supplies the valves need be only 30mm/1¼in too, unless it is particularly long.

Even if your garden is very small – consisting of a terrace, perhaps, with some beds around it and a few big plants in pots – it is still worth installing a cheap timing system to avoid disasters, such as forgetting you have left the hose turned on. In this case the controller can be a simpler one, such as the type that fixes to a garden tap and works on batteries. Your only problem then will be deciding how to hide the pipes. If you are making a terrace it is well worth laying the supply network below the paving, having planned in advance for outlets to come up in those places where you are likely to want to attach a sprinkler to water an isolated bed or a group of pots.

## SPRINKLERS

Lawn sprinklers come in a multitude of designs. The least expensive are rotary and throw a circular pattern of water. These circles must overlap, or some areas at the intersections will receive no water at all. Rather better results are achieved with sprinklers that oscillate and cover a rectangular space, but these generally have smaller holes and need more care to keep clean.

It is a good idea to start a sprinkler at the far end of the garden and use the hose to pull it towards you, to avoid walking on the area you have just watered, and having to turn off the water every time you want to move it. To work out how long you need to leave a sprinkler in one position you can put a straight-sided saucepan under the spray. Measure the depth of water in the pan at intervals: with most soils, you should aim at 20-25mm/¾-1in of water. However, some soils are not able to accept so heavy a watering in one go. With clay soils, for example, the water will simply run off and be wasted once the surface is saturated. So it is better to water heavy soils for a shorter period, leave the moisture to be absorbed and return to give a further watering. There is little point in giving much water to a sandy soil, because it cannot retain the moisture. With sandy soils, you should repeat the watering every three to five days instead of the more usual intervals of five to ten days.

The light, cheap lawn sprinklers are not suitable for

An automatic system with a control device can be used for any low-level watering. A seep hose is ideal for irrigating small plants; water oozes without disturbing the roots. Sprinklers are good for watering large areas and can be raised above obstructions. Drip emitters can be placed in a ring, at the farthest reach of the branches, to water trees.

With a system such as this, it is important to 'earth' all electrical parts. The design must include enough hand valves to isolate a section of burst or leaking pipe or a blocked electrovalve. Efficient filtration of the water will avoid blocked valves or emitters. Taps on the end of the lines will allow you to wash out the whole system occasionally.

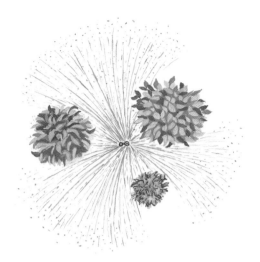

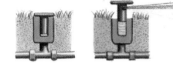

Powerful high-level sprinklers (*above*) reduce the effort of watering a large garden. Raised to a height of 1m/3ft, on top of a post or the water supply pipe, the 'throw' may well cover more than 15m/50ft, a diameter of 30m/100ft. The principal drawback is that trees and tall shrubs cast 'rain shadows' (*right above*) and receive too much water on the side facing the spray and remain dry on the far side.

With low-level pop-up sprinklers (*right*), water pressure pushes up the jet when the tap is turned on. When not in use they disappear below ground, and so are unobtrusive and less prone to damage.

watering trees, shrubs or densely planted perennials, as the foliage will interfere with the throw of the water. The solution lies with the larger type of sprayer that turns, by reaction, as a small sprung arm on the head hits the watering bar every second or so. This is a type of sprayer you often see used commercially. Such sprayers range from enormous rain guns that are capable of watering a whole field at a time to small plastic devices suitable for gardens. The advantage lies in their simplicity and in the fact that you can mount them on top of a galvanized tube, well above the surrounding foliage. They do, however, need two to three atmospheres of water pressure to operate effectively, and this often means installing a pump to drive them, a job which is best left to a specialist firm. With this kind of sprinkler it is best to water at night, when wind drift problems are at a minimum and the spray is less likely to give an unwelcome shower to anybody passing by.

The pop-up mini-sprinkler system designed originally for lawns has many advantages in the garden, but installing it is quite a big and expensive job. It has to be fed by a supply pipe buried deep enough to be well below the cultivation level. You will probably need a pump, because the pressure to the jets needs to be equivalent to at least two to three atmospheres. When the pressure is turned on, the jet pops up out of the ground and gives a circular or sectorial spray, 10-20m/30-60ft in diameter. When the watering is finished and the pressure disappears, these jets fall back into their below-ground housings and can be walked over. On the whole, this type of watering system probably gives the best results.

# SOIL

Soil performs four vital functions for a plant: it anchors the roots, and it supplies them with air, water and food. Each type of soil will fulfil some of these functions better than others.

The roots of a plant tend to be forgotten, because one so seldom sees them, but they are just as important as the trunk, stems or foliage. In any growing plant the parts above and below ground must be balanced, or the plant will grow less strongly than it might: so the huge above-ground development of a great tree requires just as large a root-system below ground, finding food and drink for the leviathan, and anchoring it down. Each root hair of this vast system needs oxygen as much as any other living tissue that makes up the plant. This surprises some people, who do not realize that air, the source of oxygen, is an essential component of healthy soil and essential for root growth. 'But how does air get to the roots?' they ask.

A major force inducing air to enter the soil is the piston effect that occurs when water, falling through the soil, draws air behind it. If you doubt the power of this effect, place one of your pot plants in a saucer full of water, and then water the soil well from the top. You should see bubbles of air, pushed out of the bottom of the pot by the descending piston of water, welling up in the saucer. The plant itself helps to oxygenate the soil, because water absorbed by the roots is replaced by the air. This partly explains why it is better to water well but infrequently, rather than little and often: a thorough watering helps the soil to breathe deeply. It is also the reason why you should always use a pot that is just larger than the root ball of the plant that it holds. In a small pot a small plant can absorb sufficient water to refresh the soil air. In a large pot it cannot: as a result, the soil can become starved of air, and the roots of the plant are likely to die.

One cannot overestimate the importance to plant life of well-aerated soil. This is why an open soil structure is ideal, and why it is beneficial to hoe and mulch the soil surface to avoid the build-up of a hard crust through which it is difficult for the air to pass.

Good soil must also be capable of holding substantial quantities of water without becoming sodden. It should be spongy in texture, providing the plant with a better reserve of water, and also with plenty of space for air to move into the soil as the water is taken up.

Fine soil particles are also an advantage. It is surface tension that holds the water in the soil and prevents too much of it from falling below the reach of the plant's roots. So the more surface area there is in a soil the better; and the finer the soil particles the more surface area there is in a given quantity of soil. That is why spongy soils with a certain clay content hold water better than sandy soils, which are well aerated but, consisting of large soil particles, lose their water supply very quickly.

The majority of a plant's nourishment is also taken in through the roots, in the form of simple salts dissolved in water and disassociated into ions. These ions tend to stick to the surface of soil particles until they are called for by the plant – another reason why the large surface area provided by soils containing some clay is especially helpful to plants.

IMPROVING THE SOIL

A visitor to the Mediterranean region in high summer might be forgiven for thinking that those barren, stony fields must be quite incapable of worthwhile cultivation. But appearances deceive and when the time comes to plough the fields it is curious how rich they suddenly look. Much of the earlier appearance of infertility is caused by rain during the late spring and early summer, which washes the good earth down, leaving the stones and pebbles proud of the surface. Although the soil has more potential than the summer visitor might imagine, at the inception of most gardens some rather expensive steps may have to be taken to improve its content and structure, particularly in spots where builders may have dumped rubble.

The first problem to tackle is that of drainage. Most stony soils overlying rock are not as poor in this respect as one might think, and can absorb light rains without difficulty. The rock below is often porous or fractured, and normal rains soon filter down through it. Problems can occur, though, when the heavy deluges that periodically swamp the scenery exceed the capacity of the land to absorb them, and they run off; if the ground is not well covered they will take some of the precious soil with them. If you have a particular problem spot, it is usually possible, using a heavy crowbar, to prise loose enough boulders to make a fairly large crater, which you can then fill with earth. Increasing the soil depth in this way will help retain the rains, and once plants become established they will stabilize the soil. In intractable cases you may have to resort to blasting, at least where you plan to plant your big trees. But this apparently herculean enterprise is not as major as it sounds, and most builders can arrange to have it done.

When it comes to improving soil structure, curiously enough the two extremes of heavy clay and light sand need much the same treatment. Both require additives that retain moisture and increase aeration. Peat and perlite are both good, but expensive. Of the two, peat is usually the more readily available from garden suppliers. Sphagnum peat, sold in large rectangular bales, is better than sedge peat, sold in sacks, which has a lower water-holding capacity. Many gardeners enthuse about the benefits of polymer granules that will absorb over 150 times their own weight in water, but when I tried them I did not feel that the results really justified their high cost.

Alternatives include spent mushroom compost, composted seaweed and grape pressings. The best pressings to use consist of the skin and pips that have been boiled as part of the alcohol-making process, for boiling kills the seeds that otherwise tend to sprout, and which may also attract rats and mice. If you can only obtain untreated pulp, straight from the presses, you should compost it before use. Heap it up to a depth of 1m/3ft and keep it wet by watering it with a hose. The pile should steam and heat a little, but not so much that it chars. Turn the compost over every few months, and by the end of the following winter, fifteen months or so

later, you will be able to spread it on all your garden beds. Spread it to a depth of 100-150mm/4-6in and dig or rotovate it into the soil. If you are in a hurry you can use it the first spring, but you may get some trouble from the germinating seeds. However, you might consider turning this to advantage by using some of the seedlings to make a vine arbour or hedge, although the grapes produced will be far from the quality of grafted varieties.

I would not recommend trying to compost ordinary garden material. In damp, temperate climates this is a useful method of recycling waste, but in hot, dry conditions you are more likely to find cinders than humus when you open the pile, unless you are prepared to water it almost daily, and the effort is hardly worthwhile. Buying a load of manure will save time and give better results.

The use of sawdust as a conditioner should be treated with caution. Sawdust derived from redwood or thuja is acceptable as the wood of both trees is resistant to decay. On the other hand, the sawdust that results from processing cheap deal or Aleppo pine rots down rapidly, and the bacteria responsible for this degeneration take valuable nitrogen out of the soil. Shredded pine bark, which rots much more slowly than sawdust, is quite useful as a soil improver, though you should still add a scattering of dried blood or hoof and horn to compensate for the nitrogen loss, especially if the bark is of the Aleppo pine.

Coarse sand and grit can be added to the soil to improve the structure and, particularly, to assist in breaking up hard, lumpy clays. But in many places this sand is limestone and should not be added to soil used for growing calcifuge plants, such as azaleas and camellias.

## CULTIVATING THE SOIL
The stony soils found in many hot, dry regions are difficult to work using a spade or fork, especially when they have been baked hard by the summer sun. To turn the earth it is best to use a heavy hoe with a hip-high haft and an adze-like double head of two spikes on one side, and a flat blade, about the width of your hand and slightly longer, on the other. With this hoe you advance, hacking at the earth.

To move earth or sand you can use a pointed shovel or a swan-necked triangular short hoe, used in concert with a two-handled basket. Facing the pile of earth or sand to be moved, you place the basket against your shins and scrape the soil down into it. If you then drop the hoe you can pick up the basket by both handles and carry the soil to wherever you want it.

The cultivation of dry, sun-baked soil requires special tools, especially if the ground is full of stones. Pointed spades are better than flat blades. A hoe with an axe-head and two prongs is best for breaking up rock-hard earth and a triangular hoe is useful for moving piles of earth and sand.

# SHADE

Many plants fail to withstand continuous exposure to heat and intense sunlight without wilting. Certainly many benefit if they are shaded from the radiation of the sun at midsummer. Shade helps to lower the ambient temperature, which, in turn, reduces the plants' requirement for water. Those plants which come from areas of relatively high humidity – such as the rain forests – also benefit from wind shelter, to prevent aerial moisture, generated by evaporation from the leaves and the soil, from being blown away.

Hedges, walls and trees all provide a degree of shelter and you will find that parts of your garden are already providing micro-climates. The shady side of an enclosed courtyard or a corner between shrubs and shaded by a tree will be protected from the sun and the wind. Covered terraces, cloisters and peristyles give protection from radiation, frosts and winds – here you can place pots of more tender plants. But if you are an adventurous gardener and want to grow plants that require more shade and humidity than is naturally available, you can, without too much expense, build a special shade house or polythene tunnel. Both these structures have the added advantage that, in winter, they provide a degree of frost protection.

The simplest form of shade house consists of no more than a lean-to built against the shaded side of a wall. Wooden poles or galvanized metal tubes may be used for the structural elements. The ceiling and walls can be made of various materials, including mats of dried heather or frames of wooden slats, both of which look natural and will last upwards of seven years. There are also several proprietary materials to choose from. The most common is black or white polythene raffia netting that lasts at least ten years. But probably the best material is a new, tightly woven cloth, made of alternate strips of aluminium and polythene, made by Ludwig Svensson of Sweden. It is expensive, needs replacing every four years and the silver colour can be obtrusive, but it is ideal for the enthusiast. As well as providing shade of the correct degree, it maintains humidity at a reasonable level, without causing condensation, and keeps out night frosts down to $-4°C/25°F$.

An alternative is to buy or build a 'poly-tunnel', which usually consists of a set of aluminium arches and cross-braces which you set into the ground and cover in aluminized material or heavy-grade polythene. A further refinement is to install an irrigation system, by suspending two 25mm/1in diameter plastic tubes from the cross bars for the whole length of the tunnel. The tubes should be fitted with micro-sprayers (see page 145) and linked to the water supply via a simple timer. If you set the timer to turn on the water for one minute every two hours from 8 a.m. to 6 p.m. the sprayers will maintain a high humidity. During winter the watering should be far less frequent, and it is also wise to install some form of heating, just sufficient to stop the temperature in the tunnel from dropping to zero on very cold winter nights.

# CHOOSING THE RIGHT PLANTS

## CLIMBERS FOR QUICK COVER
Fast-growing climbers, evergreen or deciduous, for rapid cover of pergolas, etc.

*Araujia sericofera*
*Antigonon leptopus*
*Bougainvillea*
*Clematis armandii*
*Clematis montana*
*Clytostoma callistegioides*
*Gelsemium sempervirens*
*Jasminum azoricum*
*Jasminum grandiflorum*
*Jasminum officinale*
*Jasminum polyanthum*
*Lonicera japonica halliana*
*Mandevilla laxa*
*Passiflora alatocaerulea*
*Podranea ricasoliana*
*Pyrostegia venusta (ignea)*
*Rosa×fortuniana*
*Rosa banksiae*
*Rosa wichuraiana*
*Rosa* 'La Mortola' (and many more)
*Senecio mikanioides*
*Solandra guttata*
*Solanum jasminoides*
*Tecomaria capensis*
*Thunbergia alata*
*Thunbergia grandiflora*
*Trachelospermum jasminoides*
*Vitis vinifera* (grape vine)

## CLIMBERS – SELF-CLINGING
Climbers that need no system of support other than a wall

*Campsis radicans* (Rampant, deciduous)
*Distictis buccinatoria* (Rampant, evergreen)
*Euonymus fortunei*
*Fatshedera × lizei* (Evergreen, attaches weakly)
*Ficus pumila* (Starts delicately, eventually voracious)
*Hedera* (Any)
*Hoya carnosa* (Attaches weakly)

*Macfadyena unguis-cati* (Rampant, evergreen)
*Parthenocissus quinquefolia* (Strong and as ground cover)
*Parthenocissus tricuspidata* (Strong, semi-evergreen)

## CONTAINERS
Plants for conditions where roots are restricted and confined

TREES & PALMS
*Araucaria heterophylla*
*Citrus* (most)
*Cordyline indivisa*
*Cycas*
*Ficus* (most)
*Laurus nobilis*
*Olea europaea* (olive)
*Palms* (most)
*Punica granatum*

SHRUBS & CLIMBERS
*Asparagus*
*Bougainvillea*
*Callistemon* (most)
*Camellia sasanqua*
*Ceratostigma willmottianum*
*Elaeagnus × ebbingei*
*Fatsia japonica*
*Gardenia*
*Hedera*
*Hibiscus*
*Lagerstroemia indica*
*Monstera*
*Nerium*
*Photinia*
*Phyllostachys*
*Yucca*

HERBACEOUS PLANTS & BULBS
Most bulbs especially *Agapanthus, Clivia* and *Zantedeschia*
*Catharanthus roseus*
*Pelargonium*
*Phormium tenax*
*Sansevieria*
*Strelizia*
*Vinca major*

## FRAGRANCE
Plants that add an enriching new dimension to any garden setting

*Acacia* (many)
*Aloysia triphylla (Lippia citriodora)*
*Anthemis nobilis*
*Azara microphylla*
*Buddleia* (many)
*Carissa macrocarpa*
*Cestrum nocturnum*
*Cheiranthus cheiri*
*Citrus* (all)
*Daphne* (most)
*Dianthus*
*Eriobotrya japonica*
*Escallonia rubra macrantha*
*Eucalyptus citriodora*
*Freesia × hybrida*
*Gardenia* (most)
*Heliotropium × hybridum*
*Hymenocallis narcissiflora*
*Hymenosporum flavum*
*Jasminum* (most)
*Lavandula* (most)
*Lonicera*
*Mahonia*
*Mandevilla laxa*
*Matthiola incana* (stocks)
*Nicotiana*
*Osmanthus*
*Pancratium maritimum*
*Philadelphus*
*Polianthes tuberosa*
*Rosa*
*Sarcococca*
*Sophora secundiflora*
*Thymus*
*Trachelospermum jasminoides*
*Viburnum*

## GROUND COVER
Labour-saving plants that will make a mat and subdue weeds

*Ajuga reptans*
*Arctotheca calendula*
*Aptenia cordifolia*
*Atriplex semibaccata*

Baccharis pilularis
Bougainvillea (if trained)
Carprobrotus
Cotoneaster salicifolius 'Repens'
Erigeron karvinskianus
× Fatshedera lizei
Festuca glauca
Gazania (creeping kinds)
Hedera
Helianthemum
Helichrysum petiolare
   (H. petiolatum)
Jasminum azoricum
Jasminum polyanthum
Juniperus (many)
Lantana montevidensis
Lampranthus
Limonium perezii
Liriope spicata
Lonicera pileata
Mesembryanthemum
Nepeta × faassenii
Ophiopogon japonicus
Osteospermum fruticosum (clones vary)
Pelargonium peltatum
Polygonum capitatum
Rosa banksiae
Rosa × fortuniana
Santolina chamaecyparissus
Sarcococca
Sedum
Teucrium chamaedrys
Thymus × citriodorus
Thymus vulgaris
Trachelospermum jasminoides
Vinca
Viola odorata

## GUARANTEED
Tough, self-confident plants that, given the right conditions, will grow easily

### TREES
Acacia dealbata hybrids
Acacia podalyriifolia
Albizia julibrissin rosea
Arbutus unedo
Brachychiton acerifolius
Broussonetia papyrifera
Callistemon viminalis
Celtis australis
Ceratonia siliqua
Cercis siliquastrum

Diospyros kaki
Eucalyptus camaldulensis
   (E. rostrata)
Eucalyptus gomphocephala
Ficus carica
Fraxinus uhdei
Gleditsia
Koelreuteria bipinnata
Laurus nobilis
Ligustrum lucidum
Melia azedarach
Olea europaea
Platanus × acerifolia
Populus alba pyramidalis
   (P. bolleana)
Prunus cerasifera 'Pissardii'
Punica granatum
Quercus ilex
Robinia pseudoacacia
Schinus molle
Tamarix
Ulmus parvifolia
Washingtonia filifera

### SHRUBS
Abelia × grandiflora
Artemisia arborescens
Buddleia davidii
Ceratostigma
Coronilla
Cotinus coggygria
Cotoneaster lacteus
Echium fastuosum
Elaeagnus × ebbingei
Eriocephalus africanus
Fatsia japonica
Hibiscus syriacus
Lantana hybrids
Limoniastrum monopetalum
Myoporum laetum
Nerium oleander
Pittosporum tobira
Plumbago auriculata (P. capensis)
Rosa
Teucrium fruticans
Viburnum tinus
Yucca

### CLIMBERS
Campsis grandiflora
Campsis radicans
Distictis buccinatoria
Hedera
Jasminum varieties
Macfadyena unguis-cati

Mandevilla laxa
Passiflora alatocaerulea
Podranea ricasoliana
Rosa (esp. × fortuniana &
   wichuraiana)
Tecomaria capensis
Trachelospermum jasminoides
Vitis vinifera

### HERBACEOUS
Aspidistra
Aster × frikartii
Calendula officinalis
Centaurea cineraria
Centranthus ruber
Cortaderia selloana
Dendranthema (Chrysanthemum)
Erigeron karvinskianus
Felicia
Gaillardia × grandiflora 'Goblin'
Gazania (silver creeping kinds)
Impatiens New Guinea hybrids
Iris unguicularis
Lavandula dentata
Lobularia maritima (alyssum)
Mesembryanthemum (and relatives)
Osteospermum fruticosum
Pelargonium peltatum
Pelargonium × domesticum
Pelargonium × hortorum
Petunia
Portulacaria afra
Santolina chamaecyparissus
Senecio bicolor cineraria (cineraria)
Sternbergia lutea
Tagetes (marigolds)
Thymus vulgaris
Zantedeschia aethiopica
Zephyranthes grandiflora

### HEDGES
Mainly evergreen shrubs, classed as suitable for three sizes of hedge. T (over 2m/6ft) M (1-2m/3-6ft) L (less than 1m/3ft)

Berberis M
Buxus TM
Choisya ternata M
Cotoneaster ML
× Cupressocyparis leylandii TM
Cupressus macrocarpa TM
Cupressus sempervirens TM
Elaeagnus × ebbingei M

*Escallonia* ML
*Euonymus japonica* ML
*Lavandula* L
*Ligustrum* TM
*Lonicera pileata* L
*Myoporum pictum* TM
*Myrtus communis* TML
*Pistacia* ML
*Pittosporum* M
*Pyracantha* M
*Quercus ilex* TM
*Rosa rugosa* M
*Rosmarinus officinalis* L
*Santolina chamaecyparissus* L
*Tamarix* TM
*Templetonia retusa* M
*Teucrium chamaedrys* L
*Thuja orientalis* (some) TM
*Viburnum tinus* TM
*Westringia fruticosa* L

## PATIO PLANTS FOR COLOUR
Certain to give a good display, long
flowering season as long as they are
watered regularly – perhaps daily in
summer. P (perennials) A (best used
as an annual) F (frost tender)

*Achimenes* (shade) PF
*Ageratum* A
*Amaranthus caudatus* A
*Antirrhinum* A
*Argyranthemum frutescens* P
*Begonia semperflorens* (shade) A
*Calendula officinalis* A
*Coleus* (shade) A
*Cyclamen* (shade) P
*Felicia* P
*Impatiens walleriana* New Guinea
  hybrids (half shade) A
*Impatiens walleriana sultanii* (shade) A
*Limonium perezii* PF
*Pelargonium* PF
*Pericallis × hybrida* (cineraria)
*Petunia* A
*Phlox drummondii* A
*Primula* (PP. *veris, elatior, acaulis,
  malacoides & obconica*) A
*Rudbeckia* 'Goldilocks' P
*Salvia splendens* A
*Streptocarpus* (shade) PF
*Tagetes* (TT. *erecta & patula* (African
  & French marigolds) A
*Tropaeolum majus* (nasturtium) A

*Verbena × hybrida* P
*Viola tricolor* (pansy) A
*Zinnia* (miniature kinds) A

## SILHOUETTES
Plants with an interesting shape or
dramatic form that, encouraged by
pruning, show up well against a white
wall, the sea, the sky or pale distances

*Beaucarnea*
*Erythrina crista-galli*
*Juniperus chinensis* 'Kaizuka'
*Schefflera actinophylla* (*Brassaia a.*)
*Tupidanthus calyptratus*
*Yucca elephantipes*

## SWIMMING POOL
## COMPATIBLE
Most palms, because they do not
litter. (Do not plant bamboo.)

*Abelia × grandiflora*
*Agapanthus*
*Clivia*
*Colocasia esculenta*
*Cordyline*
*Elaeagnus × ebbingei*
*Ensete*
*Fatsia japonica*
*Hemerocallis*
*Ligustrum lucidum*
*Musa*
*Phormium*
*Pittosporum tobira*
*Strelitzia nicolai*

## TREES
### COLUMNAR
*Cupressus sempervirens* (Italian cypress)
*Ginkgo biloba* 'Fastigiata'
*Juniperus scopulorum* 'Skyrocket'
*Juniperus communis* 'Hibernica'
*Koelreuteria paniculata* 'Fastigiata'
*Populus alba pyramidalis*
*Populus nigra italica*
*Robinia pseudoacacia* 'Pyramidalis'

### FAST-GROWING
*Ailanthus altissima*
*Albizia distachya*
*Arecastrum romanzoffianum*

*Eucalyptus camaldulensis*
*Eucalyptus gomphocephala*
*Fraxinus uhdei*
*Gleditsia triacanthos*
*Ligustrum lucidum*
*Myoporum laetum*
*Parkinsonia aculeata*
*Paulownia tomentosa*
*Populus* (most)
*Schinus molle*
*Tipuana tipu*

### LARGE DECIDUOUS
*Celtis australis*
*Ginkgo biloba*
*Gleditsia triacanthos* 'Sunburst'
*Jacaranda mimosifolia*
*Paulownia tomentosa*
*Platanus × acerifolia*
*Populus alba*
*Populus nigra*
*Robinia pseudoacacia*
*Sophora japonica*
*Tipuana tipu*
*Ulmus parvifolia*

### MEDIUM TO LARGE EVERGREEN
*Brachychiton acerifolius*
*Eucalyptus camaldulensis* (*E. rostrata*)
*Ficus macrophylla*
*Ficus microcarpa* (*F. retusa*)
*Fraxinus uhdei*
*Magnolia grandiflora*
*Pittosporum undulatum*

### SMALL FOR LIGHT SHADE
*Albizia julibrissin* 'Rosea'
*Catalpa bignonioides*
*Eucalyptus torquata*
*Firmiana simplex*
*Gymnocladus dioica*
*Jacaranda mimosifolia*
*Koelreuteria bipinnata*
*Lagerstroemia indica*
*Melia azedarach*
*Parkinsonia aculeata*
*Schinus molle*

### WEEPING
*Agonis flexuosa*
*Callistemon viminalis*
*Salix babylonica*
*Salix × sepulcralis chrysocoma*
*Sophora japonica* 'Pendula'
*Ulmus parvifolia*

# USEFUL ADDRESSES

Suppliers of unusual seeds suitable for sowing in a Mediterranean climate

## AUSTRALIA

H. G. Kershaw Pty Ltd
P.O. Box 84
Terrey Hills
NSW 2084
Tel: 61-2-450 2444
*Wholesalers*

Nindethana Seed Service R.M.B
939 Woogenilup
6324
Western Australia
Tel: 098 54 1006
*More than 275 Acacias and 325 Eucalypts offered*

Royston Petrie Seeds
P.O. Box 77
Dural
N.S.W. 2158
Tel: 61-2-651-2658
*Wholesalers*

## GREAT BRITAIN

Thompson and Morgan
London Road
Ipswich
Suffolk IP2 0BA
Tel: 0473 688588
Telex: 987721
*A very wide selection of flowers, shrubs, vegetable and tree seeds from all over the world*

Chiltern Seeds
Bortree Stile
Ulverston
Cumbria LA12 7PB
Tel: 0229 581137
*Another reliable supplier with a thick catalogue holding an abundance of useful information on perhaps an even longer list of plants including a high proportion of 'Mediterranean' seeds.*

## NEW ZEALAND

Peter B. Dow and Company
P.O. Box 696
Gisborne 3800
New Zealand
Tel: 079 83408
Fax 079 78844
*Has a wide range of seeds of many Australasian plants*

## SOUTH AFRICA

The Botanical Society of SA
Kirstenbosch Botanical Garden
Private Bag X7
Claremont 7735
CP
South Africa
*Many unusual trees, succulents and Mediterranean plants*

## UNITED STATES

Carter Seed Co.
475 Mar Vista Dr
Vista
California 92083
Tel: 619 724 5931
Fax: 619 724 8832

Exotic Seed Co.
Suite 125
8033 Sunset Boulevard
West Hollywood
California 90046
*Largely fruit*

Clyde Robin Seed Company
25670 Nickel Place
Hayward
CA 94545
*Many wild Californian plant seeds*

## BULB SUPPLIERS

Van Tubergen B V
P.O. Box 86
2160 Ab Lisse
Holland
Tel: 02521-19030
Telex: 41417 tuhmnl
Telegrams TUBERG-LISSE
*A very wide selection of bulb species and varieties*

## PLANT NURSERIES

Architectural plants
Cooks Farm
Nuthurst
Horsham
West Sussex RH1 6LH
Tel: 0403-891 772

Jungle Giants
Morton
Bourne
South Lincs PE10 0NW

The Palm Centre
563 Upper Richmond Rd West
London SW14 7ED
Tel: 876 3223

Two nurseries on the French Riviera with wide ranges of unusual plants of interest to the plant collector:

Schneider Soeurs
76 Avenue Maréchal-Juin
06100 Cannes
Tel: 93 43 18 55
*Shrubs, climbers and trees*

Pépinieres Michele Dental
1569 Route de la Mer
06410 Briot
Cannes
Tel: 93 65 63 32
*Small shrubs and herbaceous plants*

# BIBLIOGRAPHY

Benjamin, R. 'Gardening in a Mediterranean Climate' RHS Journal 98, 20-26: 267-270, 1973

Duffield, Mary Rose and Jones, Warren D. *Plants for Dry Climates* H.P. Books, Tucson, Arizona, 1981

Hanbury, Lady *La Mortola Garden* OUP, Oxford, 1938

Hogan, Elizabeth L. (ed.) *Sunset Western Garden Book* Lane Publishing Co., Menlo Park, California, 1988

Lord, E. *Shrubs and Trees for Australian Gardens* 4th edition, Lothian Publishing Co., Sydney, Australia, 1964

Martineau, Mrs P. *Gardening in Sunny Lands: The Riviera, California, Australia* Cobden-Sanderson, London, 1924

Maxwell, V. S. *A Simple Guide to Gardening on the Costa del Sol* 7th edition, Club de Jardineria de la Costa del Sol, 1987

New South Wales Forestry Commission *Trees for New South Wales* Sydney, Australia, 1976

# INDEX

# P

Palm, bamboo 80, Canary 80-1,
 Chinese fan 18; date 80-1; desert
 fan 83; European fan 79; fan 79;
 feather 79; lady 18; Mexican fan
 83; phoenix 27; queen 79; yatay 81
pampas grass 119
pansies *127*, 128
*Paphiopedilum* 132
Paradise Garden 12
Paris daisies 118
*Parkinsonia aculeata* 72
*Passiflora* × *alatocaerulea* 111; *caerulea*
 41; *edulis* 111; *manicata* 111, *111*
passion flower 41
passion fruit 111, *111*
paths, dry site 20; gravel *24*, 28, *33*
patio garden **17-19**, 25; roof on 18;
 surfaces for 10, 18, *18*, 28
*Paulownia tomentosa* 72
paving and hard surfaces 18, *18*, 28,
 **30-3**; courtyard 14, *14*; dry site 20;
 under raised bed 50
*Pelargonium* 22, 46, 49, 50, *122*;
 × *domesticum* 122; *graveolens* 122;
 × *hortorum* 122; *odoratissimum* 122;
 *peltatum* 122; *tomentosum* 122
pelargonium, regal 122
pepper tree 76
perennials **115ff.**; on terracing 24
pergolas *13*, *18*, 28, **38ff.**; over patio
 18, *18*: roofing for 41: on terrace 24
periwinkle, greater 123; Madagascar
 125
*Perovskia atriplicifolia* 99
*Persea americana* 72-3
persimmon 67
*Petunia* 46, 126-7, *127*
*Phaedranthus buccinatorius* 108
*Philodendron pertusum* 18, 111
*Phlomis* *115*
*Phlox drummondii* 127
*Phoenix* 80-1; *canariensis* *78*, 80-1;
 *dactylifera* 80-1; *roebelenii* 81
*Phormium cookianum* 123; *tenax* 122-3
*Photinia* × *fraseri* 99; *glabra* 99;
 *serrulata* 99
*Phyllostachys aurea* 86; *nigra* 86
pickerel weed 45
pineapple guava 84
pine trees 20, *59*, *73*, 73-4
pink, common 119; maiden 119
pink trumpet vine 112, *112*
*Pinus* 73-4; *canariensis* 73; *halepensis*
 73-4, *73*; *pinea* 74

*Pistacia lentiscus* 99; *terebinthus* 99
pistachios 20
*Pittosporum* 99-100, *115*; *tenuifolium* 74;
 *tobira* 74, 99, 100; *undulatum* 74
plane tree 24, 74
plants, choosing **51-3**; bog garden 45;
 courtyard 14; dry garden 20;
 ground cover 36; patio 18; pergola
 41; water garden 27
*Platanus* × *acerifolia* (*P.* × *hybrida*)
 24, 74
*Platycladus orientalis* 77
*Plumbago auriculata* (*P. capensis*) 100,
 *100*, *105*
*Podranea ricasoliana* 112, *112*
poinsettia 120
polyanthus 127; as annuals 115
*Polygonum aubertii* 112; *baldschuanicum*
 112; *capitatum* 123
'poly-tunnel' 149
pomegranate *14*, 75, *75*
*Pontederia cordata* 45
pools/ponds 42; raised *42-3*
*Populus alba* 74-5
*Portulacaria afra* 137
potato vine 113, *113*
pots, see containers/pots
prickly pear 137, *137*
primrose 127
primrose tree 70-1
*Primula* 127
privet 96
pruning, time for 9
*Prunus cerasifera* 74, 75; *dulcis* 75;
 *serrulata* 74, 75
*Punica granatum* *14*, 75, *75*; *granatum*
 *nana* 75
*Pyracantha* 100

# Q

*Quercus ilex* 75

# R

*Racosperma dealbatum* hybrids 58
rain lily 134
raised beds **49-50**
*Ranunculus asiaticus* 132
*Raphiolepsis* 100-1; × *delacourii* 101;
 *indica* 101
reed, common 116
*Retama monosperma* 94

rhamnus 20
*Rhapis excelsa* 18
*Robinia pseudoacacia* 75
*Romneya coulteri* 101
*Rosa* 101, 112, *114*; for pergolas 41;
 *banksiae*, 41, 112; × *fortuneana* 41,
 112; *laevigata* 112; 'Mermaid' 112;
 *rugosa* 101; *wichuraiana* 41, 112
*Rosmarinus officinalis* 101, *101*
rosemary 10, *35*, 100, *100*
rubber plant 69, *69*
*Russelia equisetiformis* (*R. juncea*)
 101-2, *102*
Russian olive 67
Russian vine 112
rye grass 36

# S

St Augustine grass 26, 34
St John's bread 62-3
*Salix alba* 76; *babylonica* 76; *babylonica
 pekinensis* (*S. matsudana*) 76;
 × *sepulcralis* 76
*Salvia splendens* 127
*Santolina chamaecyparissus* *35*, 102; as
 ground cover 36
*Sasa palmata* 86
*Schefflera arboricola* (syn. *Heptapleurum
 arboricola*) 27, 102, *102*
*Schinus molle* 76
screens 37; chain link 41. See also
 windbreaks
sea lavender 121
sea urchin tree 69
'second spring' 9
sedge 45
*Senecio mikanioides* 112-13, *115*
*Seridium cardinale* 64, 66
shade **149**; in courtyards 14; on
 terracing 24; vines for 10
shade house 149; watering 149
Shasta daisy *118*, 119
shrubs **84ff.**; around pools 27; as
 ground cover 22
silk tree 61
smoke bush 91
snapdragons 37, 125, *127*
soil **147-8**; for containers 49;
 cultivating 148, *148*; effect of
 climate on 9; effect on plant choice
 9; improving 147-8; raised bed 50
soil additives 148
*Solanum jasminoides* 113, *113*;

# ACKNOWLEDGMENTS

**Author's acknowledgments**
This book has been 'team-tailored'. Frances the 'couturière', undertook a new line. Erica ably tacked the panels. Anne has made a marvellous and skilled seamstress. Tony, Roger, Ginni and 'Kew' have ensured that the cloth hangs well – to them, and to all the others who helped at Frances Lincoln Limited, my deep thanks for all their friendly enthusiasm.

**Publisher's acknowledgments**
The publishers would like to thank the following individuals for their help in producing this book: Valerie Walley, Head of Publications, and her colleagues at The Royal Botanic Gardens, Kew; Tony Lord; Kathryn Cave, Jo Christian and Sarah Mitchell; Yvonne Cummerson for initial design work; Mike Jarvis and Peter Brealey of SX Composing who could not have been more helpful; and Niccolò Grassi for the photographs he took specially for the book.

**Photographer's acknowledgments:**
I should like to thank everyone who helped me with photography for **The Mediterranean Gardener.** I particularly wish to thank Mr William Waterfield whose beautiful garden, kind assistance and very precious help in France made my job so interesting and so much easier. I should also like to thank the owners of gardens for having kindly allowed me to photograph them. Mme and Mlle Champin, Mr Anthony Norman, Mr Raymond Poteau, Signor Guido Piacenza, Marchesa Lavinia Taverna, Contessa Maria Sanminiatelli, Signora Annalisa Moncada, Signora Benedetta Crea, Baronessa Rosanna Sanjust, Baronessa Yvone Dönhoff, Signor Mario Valentino, Signora Nina Calise, Lady Susana Walton, Principessa Maria Carla Borghese, Signora Giovannella Moncada, Signor Publisi Cosentino, Conte Lucio Tasca, Beno and Giosetta Reverdini, Angelo Naj Oleari, the Withaker Foundation, the Botanical Gardens of Naples, Palermo and Menton.

**Additional photographs:**
The following abbreviations have been use in the list below: *r* (right), *l* (left), *t* (top), *b* (bottom)
John Brookes 12 *(l)*; Inge Espen-Hansen 50 *(r)*; Derek Fell 12 *(r)*, 44, 124; Garden Picture Library/ Ron Sutherland 68; Jerry Harpur 24 (*l* Hellinger), 27 (Borum), 37 (Griot), 45 (*t* Borum), 53 (Hargreaves); Roger Hillier 94; Saxon Holt 13, 45 *(b)*; Hugo Latymer 43, 60, 65 *(tr)*, 71 *(l)*, 106 *(l)*, 111 *(r)*, 128 *(l)*, 129; Andrew Lawson 92 *(l)*; Photos Horticultural/Michael Warren 87 *(l)*, 108, 116, 130, 132, 133; Dino Scrimali 2, 11, 15, 16, 17, 18, 19, 23, 29, 34, 36, 40, 47, 50 *(l)*, 55, 80 *(b)*, 105, 115, 135, 136; Harry Smith Collection 98, 106 *(r)*, 131; EWA/ Neil Lorimer 31.

| | |
|---|---|
| Editors | Chris Catling |
| | Anne Kilborn |
| Design | Roger Walton Studio |
| Illustrator | Val Sassoon |
| Horticultural consultant | Tony Lord |
| Editorial Director | Erica Hunningher |
| Art Director | Caroline Hillier |
| Picture Editor | Anne Fraser |